DICTIONARY OF FOODS

AND
COOKERY TERMS

DICTIONARY OF FOODS

AND
COOKERY TERMS

C. Herman Senn OBE
Revised by
Harold C. Clarke MHCI

Drake Publishers Inc/New York

ISBN 877490–251–4
LCCCN 72–1256

Published in 1972 by
Drake Publishers Inc
381 Park Avenue South
New York, N.Y. 10016

Printed in Great Britain

PREFACE

IT has been a privilege to have the opportunity of revising Herman Senn's "Dictionary of Foods and Culinary Encyclopedia". In undertaking this revision I have tried not to alter the character of the original work unduly.

The primary object of this book remains the same, that is to show the reader at a glance the meaning of words applied to food, drink and cookery. As its title indicates, this book is intended to serve as a dictionary of foods and technical terms in all matters related to cookery and allied fields, many of which include foreign names. Various terms in modern usage which were not in the original volume have been included. Although an attempt has been made to make this revision as up to date as possible it is not claimed to be a complete coverage of all the vocabulary which exists in such a vast field of study.

It is my hope that this book will be as valuable as a classic reference work as the original, and of particular benefit to serious students and all those interested in good food.

HAROLD C. CLARKE

Abaisse, F. Dough crust paste. A paste thinly rolled out.

Abatis, F. The head, neck, liver, comb, kernels, and wings of a bird. Giblets.

Abats, F. Liver, lights, etc.

Abavo. Name of an Indian pumpkin, from which a delicious soup is prepared.

Abelavis. An Egyptian melon.

Abendmahl, G. Supper. Souper, F.

Able, F. A fish of the salmon kind, but somewhat smaller, found on the Swedish coast.

Ablette, F. Ablet, bleak. A very small sweet-water fish, of pink colour.

Ablette de Mer, F. Whitefish.

Abondance, F. Watered wine, Abundance.

Abricot, F. Apricot. Small fruit of the peach order.

Abricotine, F. Apricotine. A cordial or liquer.

Abricoté, F. Candied apricot. Masked with apricot marmalade.

Absinthe. A liqueur made from wormwood, a plant which has a strong aromatic smell and bitter taste. Plain absinthe is prepared with half a sherry glass of the liqueur and plenty of fine ice in about two wineglassfuls of water. The water is put, drop by drop, on the top of the liqueur and ice and stirred slowly.

Accola, IT. A marinaded fish similar to tunny fish.

Acetarious. Denoting plants used in salads.

Acetary. An acid pulp found in certain fruits.

Acetic Acid. This is an acid used in confectionery for boiled sugar goods, etc., in order to preserve whiteness, to give body or consistency, and to prevent deterioration of delicately coloured sugar work, etc. It is obtained in two forms—by the oxidisation of alcohol, wine or malt, and the distillation of organic matter, usually wood, in hermetically sealed vessels. Then known as pyroligneous acid, or crude acetic acid—dilute acetic acid has been known as vinegar since the earliest times, although vinegar, or *vin aigre* is, strictly speaking, derived from wine.

Aceto dolce, IT. Sour and sweet. A kind of Italian pickle.

Achaja. Name of a Greek wine.

Ache, F. Kind of parsley. Smallage.

Acid, F. Aigre.

Acid Curd Cheese. Made from whole, partially skimmed milk the texture of the finished cheese is dependent upon the fat content of the milk. Acid curd cheeses have a short shelf life and should be eaten within a few days of manufacture.

Acre, F. Sharp, piquante.

Admiral. A hot drink (punch), consisting of claret sweetened with sugar, flavoured with vanilla and cinnamon, and thickened with egg-yolks.

Adragant (gomme), F. Gum Tragacanth. Principal ingredient used for gum paste.

Adschempilavi. Name of a Turkish dish—consisting of pickled meat stewed with rice.

Aerated Waters. These are used as the basis of a large number of effervescing drinks, cups, etc. They are consumed alone or with wines or spirits. The process of manufacture is not difficult; they are made by forcing a certain quantity of carbonic acid into water, which, under pressure, dissolves a quantity of this gas, but gives off the greater part again as soon as the pressure is removed, or, in other words, as soon as the stopper is taken out of the bottle. Soda and potash waters should contain from 10 to 15 grains of bicarbonate of soda or potash, in addition to the carbonic acid. Seltzer water should contain chlorids of sodium, calcium, and magnesium, with phosphate and sulphate of sodium. Lemonade and other fruit beverages are made by the addition of a certain quantity of fruit essence or syrup to aerated water. There are also numerous natural mineral or aerated waters, which are obtained from springs containing certain salts in addition to carbonic acid gases. Among these may be mentioned Apollinaris, Johannis, Seltzers, Rossbach, Vichy waters, etc.

A.F.D. Accelerated freeze-drying. A process of dehydration which has been successfully applied to meat, fish, vegetables and some fruits. During the A.F.D. process ice crystals are removed by sublimation, under conditions of very low

2

pressure. The products remain stable if kept dry and protected from air; when soaked in water they regain original shape and flavour.

Affriolé (-e), F.   Appetising.

Affrité (-e), F.   Ready to fry.

Africaine (à l').   African style. Garnish: Egg plants, flap mushrooms and tomatoes are featured.

Africains.   Small French dessert biscuits.

Agaric, F.   A species of mushroom, of which there are six varieties used as edibles.

Agneau, F.   Lamb. A young sheep.

Agras, F.   A Continental drink made of pounded almonds and the juice of unripe grapes, slightly sweetened. It is served in a half-frozen condition.

Agriote, F.   Wild Cherry.

Aigre, F.   Sour or acid.

Aigre-douce Sauce (Agro-dolce).   A sweet-sharp sauce, made with vinegar, sugar, pine kernels, almonds, chocolate, and small currants; served hot.

Aigre au Cédrat, F.   A favourite beverage of Cardinal Richelieu. Orangeade flavoured with the juice of mulberries. acidulated with lemon juice, and sweetened with honey.

Aigrefin, Aiglefin, or Eglefin, F.   (*See* HADDOCK.)

Aigrelet (-ette), F.   Sharp, sour.

Aigrette, F.   Sour, piquante, also name given to small cheese fritters.

Aiguillettes, F.   Small strips of cooked meat. Breasts of ducks and geese are carved "*en aiguillettes*." Small fillets of fish, as "*Aiguillettes de Sole*."

Aiguille-à-Brider.   Larding-needle, used for inserting strips of fat bacon into lean meat or birds (breasts of).

Ail, F.   Garlic—"*une gousse d'ail*," a clove of garlic; "*une pointe d'ail*," a little on the point of a knife.

Aile, F.   The wing of a bird.

Ailerons, F.Small wings of birds; fins of some fish. Sometimes used for garnishing dishes, or served as ragoût.

Aillade, F.   Garlic condiment, sauce, or pickle.

Aine, F.   Top of sirloin.

Airelle rouge, F.   Red bilberry; dark red berries used for compôte, jellies, and marmalade; cranberry.

Airelle Myrtille, F.   Whortleberry. Huckleberry. There are two sorts. One originates in America, and is very savoury,

3

and is eaten freshly picked with savoury milk or a cream sauce. The other kind of whortleberry is a small fruit, of dark blue colour, seasoning certain dishes. Wine merchants use it to colour white wine, hence its French name *teint-vin*.

Aiselle, F.   A species of beetroot; used as vegetable or in salads.

Aitchbone of Beef. Culotte, F.   An economical joint used as boiled meat or stews. The joint lies immediately under the rump. It is a bone of the rump, which in dressed beef presents itself in view edgewise; hence it is sometimes called "edgebone," the ancient name for aitchbone. The aitchbone is not readily obtainable owing to a decline in popularity during World War II.

Ajouter, F.   To add or mix; ajoutées — applied to small garnish or side dishes served with vegetable course.

à la, F.   *à la mode*, denoting the style or fashion of a dish; *à la française*, French style; *à la Reine*, Queen style; *à l'Impératrice*, Empress style; *à la Russe*, Russian style, etc. In this sense, the feminine singular *à la* (or *à l'*, before a vowel) is always used as it refers to *mode*, which is feminine.

à la Broche, F.   Roasted in front of the fire on a spit or skewer. Nowadays it also applies to the cooking of poultry and joints of meat on electrically heated and rotated spits.

à la Diable, F.   Devilled; seasoned with hot or pungent condiments or spices.

à la Ficelle, F.   Tied with string.

à l'Huile, F.   Done in oil or served with oil, vinaigrette, etc.

Alberge, F.   Small peach.

Albran, Alebran, or Halbran, F.   Young wild duck; after the month of October it is called *canardeau*, and the month following *canard*.

Albuféra, F.   A lake near Valencia in Spain. Marshal Suchet was made "*Duc d Albuféra*" in 1812. Dishes with this name are served with a sharp brown sauce flavoured with port or madeira. A Sauce Albuféra is also made with a *Sauce Supreme* finished with pimentoes.

Albumen, Albumine, F.   A nitrogenous substance contained in white of egg and lean meat, principally beef

Alcarazas, F.   Water cooler.

Alcool, F.   Alcohol.

Alderman's Walk. The name given to the centre cut (long

incision) of a haunch of mutton or venison, where the most delicate slices are to be found. It also denotes the best part of the under-cut (fillet) of a sirloin of beef. The name is supposed to be derived from a City Company's dinner, at which a City Alderman showed a special liking for this cut.

Alénois, Cresson d'. Small garden cress.

Algérien (-ne) (à la), F. Algerian style. Garnish: sweet potatoes are usually featured.

Aliment, F. Food or food product.

Alise or **Alize,** F. Shad-apple.

Allemande (à l'), F. German style. As a surname to dishes is applied in many cases where the origins of the preparations are in a manner peculiar to Germany. Thus a dish garnished with sauerkraut and pork (pickled and boiled), its style is termed à l'Allemande. Again, a dish garnished with potato quenelles or smoked sausages may be defined in the same manner.

Allemande Sauce, F. A white reduced velouté sauce, made from veal stock, thickened with flour, cream, yolk of egg, and seasoned with nutmeg and lemon juice.

Allerlei. Name of a German dish, consisting of stewed early spring vegetables. A kind of macédoine of vegetables, principally served at Leipzig.

Alliance (à la St.), F. Name of a garnish for entrées, consisting of braied carrots, artichoke bottoms, and small onions.

Allspice. Piment, épice, F. Also called Jamaica pepper, and pimento. Allspice, like many other trade terms, is mostly a conventional one, perhaps so called on account of its composite aromatic flavour. The ground, ripe, and dried berries of a pretty evergreen-tree of the myrtle species, which grows plentifully in Jamaica. It is called "all-spice" because its flavour and smell resemble very closely that of a combination of three chief spices—cloves, cinnamon, and nutmeg. The berries when ripe and dry are somewhat similar to black pepper, only rather larger and less pungent in taste.

Allumette, F. Match, strip, e.g., pommes allumettes.

Almavica, IT. An Italian sweet dish, similar to semolina pudding.

Almond. Amande, F. A greatly appreciated fruit, used for a variety of culinary preparations, more especially sweet dishes and for dessert. The fruit of a tree resembling the peach-

5

tree. It is largely cultivated in Spain, the south of France, and Italy. There are two kinds, the sweet and the bitter. Malaga and Valentia cultivate the best sweet almonds (called Jordan almonds). Those imported from Malaga are the best. The almond is valuable for medicinal purposes as well as in the kitchen.

Alose, F. (*See* SHAD.)

Alouette, F. Or mauviette. (*See* LARK.)

Aloyau, F. Sirloin of beef. Short loin of beef. (*See also* SIRLOIN).

Alphabétique, F. Paste letters used in soups, etc.

Alphénic, F. White barley sugar, or sugar candy.

Alsacienne (à l'), F. Alsatian style. A meat garnish consisting of mashed peas, slices of ham, and smoked sausages. Foie-gras or sauerkraut may also be featured.

Alum. A salt of astringent and acid flavour. Chemically it is double sulphate of potash and alumina. It is often used in the process of sugar-boiling, especially for pulled sugar used for ornamental purposes. A tiny pinch usually suffices for a pound of sugar.

Alum Whey. An invalid drink made from milk, ½ pint, a tablespoonful wine, a teaspoonful alum, and sugar to taste.

Amalgamer, F. Amalgamate. To mix several substances.

Amande, F. (*See* ALMOND.)

Amandes (Pâté d'), F. Almond paste. A mixture of powdered almonds, sugar, and whites of eggs or water, made into a paste. Used for cake-covering, etc. *Amandes douces*—sweet almonds. *Amandes pralinées*—burnt almonds.

Amarante, F. Amaranth (a kind of spinach).

Ambigu, F. A buffet lunch. A meal where the meat and sweets are served at the same time.

Ambroisie, F. Name of a cold drink of milk, with vanilla or kirschwasser flavouring.

Ameaux, F. A kind of pastry made of puff paste and eggs.

Amer, Amère, F. Bitter.

American Fruit Pie. A flan ring lined with sweet or short paste, fruit filling in the centre, covered with paste and baked.

Américaine (à l'), F. Applied to game served with a sauce of which black-currant jelly forms a principal ingredient. Also applicable to dishes which include tomatoes and sometimes bacon. It is also the name of a lobster sauce—*Sauce Américaine.*

Amidon, F. Starch. A white farinaceous substance, obtained by a peculiar process from flour or potatoes. It is slightly soluble in cold water, but quickly melts in boiling water, and through cooling it becomes a mass similar to jelly, and is then called EMPOIS in French (or stiffened starch).

Amilacé (-e), F. Starchy.

Amiral (à l'), F. Admiral style. Name of a garnish, principally for fish, consisting of fried oysters mussels, sliced lobster fillets, and Nantua sauce. Name also adopted for meat dishes and sweet entremets.

Amontillado, F. Term applied to sherry from its eighth to fourteenth year.

Amourettes, F. Marrow cut in strips and crumbed. Lambs' fry.

Amphitryon, F. Host.

Ananas, F. Pineapple, A dessert fruit of noble appearance possessing a most delicate and delicious flavour.

Anchois, F. Anchovy, Sardellen, G. A small fish, native to the Mediterranean.

Anchovy. Though caught as far as the Black Sea, this fish is also obtained from the coasts of France, Portugal, Spain, and the British Channel, The Gorgona fish are considered the best, while the Dutch, Russian, and Norwegian varieties are distinguished by having no scales. Gorgona anchovies are imported both in brine and in oil, the Dutch in brine only. the Russian in brine and highly spiced vinegar, the Norwegian in spiced brine.

Anchovy essence. This is available in bottles and is used to add flavour to certain sauces.

Ancienne (à l'), F. Old style. A garnish, consisting of kidney beans, hard-boiled eggs, and braised cabbage lettuces. A Fricassée à l'Ancienne is garnished with button mushrooms and button onions.

Andalou (-ouse) (à la), F. Andalusian style. Characterized mainly by pimentoes, tomatoes, egg-plants and rice pilaff.

Andouille, F. Literally a hog's pudding; a kind of French sausage made of pork.

Andouillettes, F. Forcemeat balls. A kind of small sausage. A salpicon of poultry or game wrapped in pigs' caul and fried.

7

Anesse (Lait d'), F.   Ass's milk.

Aneth, F.   Dill.

Ange, F.   Angel. A fish of the shark or dog-fish family.

Angelica. Angélique, F.   The name of a green fruit-rind used in the kitchen, the tender tubular stems of which, after being preserved with sugar, are used for the purpose of decorating and flavouring sweet dishes.

Angelot.   Kind of German cheese.

Angels on Horseback.   Anges à cheval. Huîtres en cheval, F. A savoury. Oysters rolled in bacon slices, grilled, and served on toasted or fried bread *croûtes*.

Anglaise (à l').   English style. Usually implies something plain, roast or plain boiled, or that the dish is prepared in a style typical of this country.

Angleterre, F.   England.

Angloise, F.   A kind of plum tart.

Angobert, F.   A large cooking pear.

Angostura.   Probably the best known brand of bitters. It has a basis of rum which is infused with herbs and roots.

Angoumois, F.   A variety of apricot. Named after an old province of France.

Anguille, F.   (*See* EEL.)

Anguille au Gratin, F.   Eels au Gratin.

Animelles, F.   Lamb's fry.

Anis, F.   Anise or Aniseed. Aromatic plant, used for flavouring sweet puddings, creams, and pastries. In Germany it is used as one of the ingredients in a fancy bread called Anisbrod. The anise plant is a native of Egypt and China. *Aniser*—to strew over the aniseed, or to mix with aniseed. *Anisette*—aniseed cordial, E. A liqueur.

Annadas.   Term applied to young or first year's sherry.

Année, F.   Year.

Anon, F.   A fish similar to the whiting.

Antenois, F.   Yearling lamb or veal.

Antilope, F.   Antelope.

Antique, F.   Ancient.

Apfel, G.   Apple. Pomme, F.

Api, F.   (*See* POMME D' API.)

Appareils, F.   Culinary term for prepared mixtures. Preparations for an event.

Appetissant, F.   Appetising; something to whet the appetite;

8

relishing. A *hors d'oeuvre,* consisting of stuffed Spanish olives, dressed on little *croûtes* of fried bread.

Appetit, F.   Appetite. The psychological factor which causes a flow of gastric juices. Appetite is related to previous sensations of smell and taste of food. Hunger has a painful quality whilst appetite is pleasurable. The great Carême, who was for a time chef to the Prince Regent in England, used to discuss matters of gastronomy daily with his royal master. One day the Prince said, "Carême, you will make me die of indigestion, for I long to eat of everything you send to table; everything is so tempting." "Sire," answered Carême, "my business is to provoke your appetite, it is not for me to regulate it."

Apple. Pomme, F. Apfel, G.   The original apple of this country is the crab, which is astringent and bitter. There are about three hundred kinds of apple now cultivated.

Apple Brandy.   Distilled cider.

Apple Fool.   A purée of apples (apple pulp) flavoured with cinnamon; clove and sugar, mixed with whipped cream and served in glass dishes or goblets.

Apple Hedgehog.   Name of a dish of stewed apples (whole), the centres of which are filled with jam, arranged in the form of a hedgehog, decorated with shreds of almonds, covered with icing sugar, and browned in the oven.

Apple Meringue.   This is similar to apple snow, but is baked in a slow oven after being dressed on the dish.

Apple Pupton.   A kind of apple pudding made with apple pulp, breadcrumbs, butter, eggs, and sugar, baked in a plain mould, and served with a fruit syrup (hot).

Apple Snow.   A sweet consisting of apple purée covered with a layer of meringue and baked and served hot.

Apple Tansy.   This is a kind of apple fritter or omelet. The batter is made of cream and eggs, and poured over partially-stewed apples. These fritters are fried in butter, and served very hot.

Apprête, F.   Sippet; narrow slice of bread.

Apprêté, F.   Prepared, cooked, dressed.

Après-diner, F.   After dinner, afternoon, evening.

Après-midi, F.   Afternoon.

Après-souper, F.   After supper, evening.

Apricot. Abricot, F. Aprikose, G.   First introduced in England about 1562. A delicious fruit, most favoured as dessert fruit; also largely used for tarts, jam, marmalade, and jelly. The apricot-tree was introduced into Europe by Alexander the Great. A peculiarity of the tree is that it produces flowers before it bears leaves.

Aqua d'Oro, IT. A high-class liqueur invented by the Italians in the thirteenth century. It was first introduced into France in 1533 by Catherine de Medici, who became the wife of Henry II. The predominant flavour of this liqueur is rosemary and rosolio (*q.v.*)

Aquavit, F. A strong colourless spirit, distilled from potatoes and flavoured with carrawayseeds.

Arabique, F. Arabic.

Arachide, F. Earthnut; peanut.

Arac, F. Arrack. A spirit distilled from rice, palm juice or sugar-cane; principally in India and Russia.

Arbousse, F. A kind of water-melon; a native of Astrachan.

Arête, F. Fishbone.

Argenté (-e), F. Silvered or silver-plated.

Argenteuil, F. Name of a district in France, Dep. *Seine-et-Oise,* celebrated for asparagus, *Asperges d'Argenteuil.* Therefore dishes with this name usually include asparagus.

Argentine, F. Name given to various small fish with brilliant or silvery scales.

Arille, Aril, F. Mace.

Arles, F. A town in France (*Bouches du Rhone*), celebrated for its sausages, *saucissons d'Arles.*

Armagnac, F. A French brandy from the district of that name.

Arménien (-enne) (à la), F. Armenian style.

Aroma. Arome, F. Aromatic quality.

Aromates, F. Vegetable herbs as used for flavouring. Aromatic herbs, such as thyme, bay leaves, tarragon, chervil, etc. *Aromatiser,* F.—To flavour with spice or savoury herbs. Aromatic seasoning.

Aromatic Seasoning. Epice culinaire, F. A special blend of various herbs and condiments.

Aromatique, F. Aromatic.

Arrack. A spirituous liquor, usually prepared from the sweet sap of the palm tree. In common use in India, Ceylon and other Eastern countries. An inferior kind made from fermented rice.

Arroche, F. French spinach.

Arroser, F. To baste with gravy, sauce, oil, butter or dripping.

Arrowroot. Fecule de marante, F. Flour produced from the root of an American tropical plant, and used for thickening sauces, etc. The South American natives extracted a poison for their arrows from the bark of the root; hence the English name.

Artichauts (Fonds d'), F. Artichoke bottoms.

Artichoke. Artichaut, F. (*See* CHINESE, JERUSALEM, and GLOBE ARTICHOKE.)

Artois, F. Old province of France (*Pas de Calais*). Several dishes are called after this name. (*See* DARTOIS.)

Arza. An Arabian brandy from mares' milk.

Ashet. Scotch word for a dish, derived from *Assiette*.

Asiatique, F. Asiatic.

Asparagus. Asperges, F. An edible plant, originally a wild sea-coast plant of Great Britain. In season from April till end of July. It grows abundantly in the temperate regions of both hemispheres, and is found in the tropics of gigantic size. *Asparagine,* F.—The active medicinal principle of asparagus, used in medicine.

Aspic, F. Savoury jelly; *à l'aspic,* or *en aspic,* set in aspic, or garnished with aspic jelly. Aspic is clarified stock fortified with meat or fish and vegetable flavourings, rendered gelatinous with calf's feet or gelatine. Used for cold entrées, for cold savouries, and for masking and garnishing.

Assaisonnement, F. Seasoning, condiment, sauce. *Assaisonner,* F.—To season, to mix.

Assiette, F. A plate. A French term for *hors d'oeuvre,* which a plate is large enough to hold.

Assistant Cook. Aide de Cuisine, F.

Assorti, F. Assorted (as *gâteaux assortis*).

Assyrien -(enne) à (la), F. Assyrian style.

Astrachan or **Astrakhan.** Russian province. Name of a caviare, the best of its kind, exported from that place. (*See* also CAVIARE.)

Atelets, F. (*See* HATELET.) Small silver or wooden skewers used for decorative purposes.

Athénienne (à l'), F. Athenian style. Larded, braised, and garnished with fried egg-plants, served with *sauce Madère.*

Athérine, F. Sand-smelt, E. A species of fish similar to smelts, distinguishable from the real smelt by the absence of the cucumber smell so peculiar to the latter. Sand-smelts are often passed for real smelts, and though not so fine in flavour and taste they are found to be both delicate and wholesome.

Athol Brose. A Scotch drink, composed of whisky, honey, etc.

Attereaux. (*See* HATÊREAU.)

Auberge, F.   An inn.

Aubergine, F.   A garden plant. Egg-plant, a melongena. Other varieties are called egg-apple, mad-apple, and brinjaul. It is egg-shaped, and either white, yellow, or violet in colour. It is a native of the West Indies. The aubergine is an annual plant, seldom more than two feet in height, and can be cultivated in temperate regions under favourable conditions.

Aubergiste, F.   An inn-keeper; hotel-keeper. à l'-inn-keeper's style.

Auflauf, G.   Soufflé or puff; omelet, or baked soufflé pudding.

au, aux, F.   With; *au riz*—with rice; *aux champignons*—with mushrooms, etc.

au Beurre, F.   With butter or done in butter, tossed or sautéed.

au Beurre noir, F.   With black or nut brown butter.

au blanc, F.   Cooked white, white sauce.

au bleu, F.   A culinary term applied to fish simmered in salted water, seasoned with vegetables, herbs, and white wine or vinegar. Fresh water trout cooked in this manner, i.e.; *truite au bleu* is the best known example.

au brun, F.   Done in brown sauce.

au four, F.   Baked or done in the oven.

au gras, F.   French term for meat cooked and dressed with a very rich gravy or sauce.

au gratin, F.   A term applied to certain dishes prepared with sauce, garnish, and breadcrumbs, and baked brown in the oven or under the grill; served in the dish on which baked.

au jus, F.   A term for dishes of meat dressed with their juice or gravy.

au kari, F.   Curried.

au lait, F.   With milk or cooked in milk.

au maigre, F.   An expression used for dishes prepared without meat. Lenten dishes.

au naturel, F.   Applied to food cooked plainly and in very simple fashion.

au poivre vert, F.   Flavoured with green pepper (available as a paste in tins), mainly applicable to grilled beef steaks.

au rouge, F. Served with or finished in red sauce.

au vert, F. Served with or in green sauce.

Aumelette. Synonym of omelette.

Aurore, F. A yellow pink in colour, E. A culinary expression for dished up high. A garnish consisting of stuffed eggs, quartered, bread croûtons, and Aurore sauce. *Aurore sauce* consists of Allemande or Béchamel and tomato sauce, flavoured with chili vinegar and dice of mushrooms.

Autoclave, F. Large steaming vessel or steam retort.

Autrichien (-enne) (à l'), F. Austrian style. Paprika pepper is usually featured, sour cream, fennel and onion may also be included.

Autruche, F. Ostrich.

Auvernat, F. Orleans wine.

Avant-Goût, F. Foretaste.

Aveline, F. (*See* FILBERT.)

Avi (à l'). Burnt.

Avignon. A city of gastronomic fame in France.

Avocado pear (Alligator pear). Avocat, F. The fruit of the Avocado tree, native of Tropical and sub-tropical areas, particularly America. It is usually pear shaped and is a greenish or purple colour. Avocado pears may be eaten plain, served with vinaigrette sauce; or the centre can be filled with prawns, shrimps, etc.

Avoine, F. Oats, E. *Crême d'avoine*—cream of oats. Used for soups and puddings.

Avola. Name of Sicilain town renonwed for its sweet almonds.

Azy, F. Rennet made of skimmed milk and vinegar.

Azyme, F. Unleavened bread.

Baba (from the Polish word babka). A very light yeast cake of flour, butter, milk and eggs, flavoured with lemon, rum or kirsch, and usually containing currants, a substitute for tipsy cake.

Baba au Rhum. Rum cake.

Babawte. A South African dish. A baked curry of minced beef.

Babeurre, F. Buttermilk.

Babka. Name of a Polish-Russian Cake. Prepared as a custard, containing fruit, almonds, etc.

Bacalao. Name of a Spanish fish speciality, consisting usually of salt cod, with a savoury dressing.

Bacardi. A well known brand of rum.

Backings. Name of a kind of fritter, best known in America, where they form a highly-esteemed dish for breakfast.

Bacon. Lard, F. The sides of a pig salted and smoked. Smoked bacon—*lard fumé*. Larding bacon, *see lard à piquer*.

Bael or **Bengal Quince.** A fruit of the orange tribe. Highly esteemed in India as a preserve, either as jam or as a syrup.

Bagasse, F. Sugar cane.

Bagration, F. Name applied to certain high-class dishes, notably a soup. Bagration was a Russian count, whose chef was the celebrated A. Carême.

Baie de Ronce, F. (*See* BLACKBERRY, E.)

Bain-Marie, F. The culinary water-bath. It is a large open vessel, half-filled with hot water, where sauces, etc., are kept in small saucepans, so that they are nearly at the boiling point without burning or reducing.

Baisers, F. Kisses; a kind of sweets. *Baisure,* F.—Kissing crust (the soft part where two loaves of bread are attached).

Baissière, F. Wine sediment.

Baisure, F. Delicate crust.

Baking. A common form of cooking by means of dry heat. The term "baking" is usually applied when articles are cooked in an oven or some other close structure, in which the action of the dry heat is more or less modified by the presence of steam which arises from the food whilst cooking. Bread has been baked from immemorial antiquity. Lot baked unleavened bread more than three thousand six hundred years ago; Pharaoh had his baker; and in the ceremonial law given by Moses to the ancient Jews, they were distinctly directed to bring cakes "baken in the oven".

Baking Powder. Poudre de Levure, F. Raising agent used in baking cakes, pastry, etc.

Balantier, F Wild pomegranate.

Bâle. Basle. A Swiss city famous for its honey cakes. "Leckerlies."

Ball Supper, E. Souper de Bal, F.

Balle, F. Ball.

Ballotine, F. Small balls or rolls of meat or fowl.

Bamboo shoots. The young shoots of an edible bamboo plant which are slightly acid. They may be boiled or fried and are similar in flavour to the artichoke; also available in tins.

Banana, E. Banane, F. Fruit of the plantain-tree. Used as dessert fruit; also for puddings, creams, ices, fritters, etc. This fruit forms one of the principal sources of food in the tropics. It is eaten raw when ripe, when unripe can be boiled and served as a vegetable, or baked and served with orange juice. The banana of to-day differs as widely from its ancestors as does the potato.

Bannocks (Scotch). A kind of thin, round, flat cake, made with oatmeal, butter, baking powder, and water. They are baked like griddle cakes, on a hot iron or in a frying-pan. Finally, they are toasted till quite crisp.

Banquet, F. A sumptuous feast; an entertainment of eating and drinking. *Banqueter,* F.—To banquet, to feast, to treat oneself to a good feast.

Bantam Fowl. A very small fowl, so called because it was originally brought from Bantam, Indonesia. It is now largely bred in this country. Bantam eggs, though small, are of superior quality.

Bar rayé, F. Striped bass.

Bar de Mer, F. Sea bass.

Baraquille, F. A large pie made of rice, chicken, and truffles.

Barbe, F. Beard; wattle (of a turkey, etc.); fin (of flat fish); "mould" on preserves.

Bar, F. (*See* BASS.)

Barbeçue, F. The mode of cooking (roasting) an animal whole; a social entertainment in the open air; to dress and roast whole. It also refers to occasions when smaller items, e.g.: steaks, sausages, joints of chicken etc., are cooked over an open fire outdoors.

Barbe de Bouc, F. A plant resembling the salsify. It is boiled in seasoned water or stock, or baked.

Barbe de Capucin, F. Monk's beard. (*See also* CHICORY.)

Barbe de Jupiter, F. House-leek, a plant with succulent leaves that grows on walls and cottage roofs.

Barbel, Barbeau, F. A fish of the carp family. This fish is seldom eaten in England; but in some parts of the Continent it is often found and appreciated.

Barberry. A small fruit resembling the black currant both in size and colour. Largely used for preserves, jellies, and pickles; the flavour being rather acid it is not eaten raw.

Barbillon, F. Young barbel.

Barboteur, F. Tame duck.

Barbotte, Barbot or **Burbot** is the common name for Lotte or Eelpout.

Barbottes en Casserole, F. Stewed eel-pout. (*See* CASSEROLE.)

Barbue, F. (*See* BRILL.)

Barcelonas. Small kiln-dried Spanish nuts.

Barcolé (-e), F. Speckled.

Barder, F. To bard. To cover breasts of game or poultry with thin slices of bacon fat.

Barigoule (é la). Style of garnish applied to artichokes, served with a brown sauce and coarsely-minced mushrooms.

Baril, F. Small barrel.

Bar-Le-Duc, F. Lorraine fruit preserve or jelly.

Barley. Orge, F. Pearl barley—*orge mondé,* F. Barley bread—*pain d'orge,* F. Barley soup—*crême d'orge,* F. Barley water—*eau d'orge,* F. Barley sugar—*sucre d'orge,* F.

Barm. Yeast. Levain, F. The scum of malt liquor.

Baron. Double loin of beef. Saddle of mutton or lamb with legs attached. *Baron of Beef*—a very large joint of the ancient kitchen. It consists of both sides of the back, or a double sirloin, and weighs from 40 to 100 lbs. It is always roasted, but is now rarely prepared, except at some festive occasions of the English Court, or at some great public entertainment.

Barquette, F.　A small boat. A boat-shaped piece of pastry, etc.

Bar noir, F.　Black bass, E.

Barsez.　A Polish soup made of beetroot.

Bartavelle, F.　French partridge. Red partridge.

Basil, Basilic, F.　An aromatic pot herb, allied to thyme. Basil vinegar is made by steeping the leaves in vinegar, and is used for flavouring when the fresh plant cannot be procured.

Basler Leckerli.　Bâle delicacy. A kind of dessert cake, is richly flavoured with honey and spice, called after the town of Bâle, where they are mostly made. These delicacies are to be found at almost every railway buffet on the Continent.

Basque.　Gascogne—famous for its cookery.

Bass, Bar, F.　A fish belonging to the same order as the perch. It is sometimes called white salmon, or salmon-dace. It attains a weight of fifteen pounds, but it is usually much smaller.

Basse-pâte, F.　Under crust.

Basse rayée, F.　Striped bass.

Basse de Mer, F.　Sea bass.

Bassin, F.　Shallow dish or large plate.

Bassine, F.　Deep pan or basin.

Baste—to baste.　To drip or pour liquefied fat on meat during the process of roasting, in order to prevent the outside of joints, birds, etc., from becoming dry.

Bath Chap.　The cheek and jaw-bone of the pig, salted and smoked. Thus called because those coming from Bath were first known, and the first to obtain a reputation as being the very finest.

Bâton, F.　Stick or slice. *Bâtons royaux,* F.—Small patties of minced chicken and game; the favourite dish of Charles XII.

Batter.　Pâte ᴮ frire, F.　A light frying batter.

Batterie de Cuisine, F.　A complete set of cooking utensils and apparatus.

Baudruche, F.　Sausage casing.

Bavarois (-e) (à la), F.　Bavarian Style.

Bavarois au Marasquin.　Bavarian cream with maraschino flavour.

Bavarois, F.　Bavarian cream, E.—A kind of cold custard

cream. Made with almond milk, eggs, sugar, cream and gelatine.

Bavarois à l'Eau, F. Tea flavoured with syrup of *capillaire* and orange-flower water.

Bavette d'Aloyau. Thin flank of skirt of beef or veal.

Bayleaf. Laurier, F. The leaf of a species of the laurel-tree, known as the cherry laurel. Largely used as flavouring. It is generally included in the *bouquet garni*. Bayleaf flavour should always be used in moderation. It is extensively employed in Sweden and Russia in the preserving of anchovies and other fish.

Bayonnaise (à la). Garnished with anchovy, fillets, gherkins, and braised button onions.

Beans, French. Haricots verts, F. Broad beans—*Féves*. Green kidney beans—*Flageolets*. String beans mixed with flageolets—*haricots panachés*. (*See also* FASCOLE and FAYOL.)

Bèche de Mer. (*See* TREPANG.)

Béarnaise, F. Name of a rich buttery herb sauce with yolk of egg thickening. Comes from the word Béarn, birthplace of King Henry IV., who was a great gourmand.

Beauvilliers (Antoine). Name of a clever cuisinier, born 1754, died 1871. Created one of the first restaurants in Paris. Palais Royal Restaurant was first opened by him. Author of "L'Art du Cuisinier," a standard work of that period.

Becare, F. Roe salmon.

Bécasse, F. Woodcock. *Bécasseau*—sandpiper; a young woodcock. *Bécassine*—snipe.

Bécasses rôties, F. Roast woodcock.

Béchamel or **Béchamelle,** F. French white sauce. Recognised as one of the four foundation sauces. Named after its supposed inventor, the Marquis de Béchamel, who acted as steward in the service of King Louis XIV. *Morue à la Béchamel, sauce béchamelle* (which see).

Bécune, F. Sea pike.

Beef. Bœuf, F. Boiled beef—*bœuf bouilli*. Roast beef—*bœuf rôti*. Braised beef—*bœuf braisé*. Beef has from time immemorial been esteemed as the most substantial food. Its mode of cooking is usually of the simplest kind, though an infinite variety of dishes are made from it.

Beefburger. A mixture of minced beef, onion and seasoning shaped into a thin medallion and cooked on a griddle plate or shallow fried.

18

Beef-tea. The essence of beef, extracted by a slow process of cooking, more or less diluted, as required.

Beer. Bière, F. Bier, G. A beverage made of malt and hops. Infusion of malt, flavoured with the bitter of hops, fermented with yeast, First known by the ancient Egyptians, from whence it was brought to the Greeks, Romans, and Gauls. A Roman historian mentions this beverage as being in daily use under Julius Cæsar (about the beginning of the Christian Era).

Beetroot. Betterave, F. A saccharine root. A wholesome and nutritious vegetable largely used pickled for salads and as garnish: it is extensively used for the manufacture of sugar. It forms a delicious salad, and makes an excellent soup. Beetroot leaves are useful as a vegetable, they are cooked the same as spinach.

Béhague, F. Name given to Southdown mutton or mutton raised on the salt marshes of France. Also termed pré-salé, the name is derived from the Marquis de Béhague, one of the great French sheep farmers.

Beignets, F. Fritters. Anything dipped in batter or thin paste and fried in deep fat.

Beignets de Crème Frites, F. Cream fritters.

Beignets de fromage, F. Cheese fritters; made from choux paste to which cheese is added.

Beignets d'Huitres, F. Oyster fritters.

Beignets de Pêches, F. Peach fritters.

Beignets de RIs de Veau, F. Sweetbread fritters.

Beignets soufflés, another name for *pets de nonnes* (*q.v.*). These are fritters of choux paste, served with a sweet sauce, e.g.: apricot sauce.

Bellevue (à la or en), F. Popular title applied to cold entrées (poultry) masked with white chaudfroid sauce, garnished with truffles, tongue, tarragon leaves, and chopped aspic jelly.

Bénédictine. A liqueur largely used for flavouring purposes, originally made by Benedictine monks.

Berçy, F. There are two sauces with this name, both of which include a reduction of white wine; a white fish sauce and a brown sauce served with grilled meats.

Bergamotte or **Bergamot,** F. A species of pears, with a very agreeable flavour.

Bergère, F. Shepherdess.

Berlingot, F. A kind of caramel sweetmeat.

Berlinois, F. A kind of light yeast cakes in the shape of balls similar to dough-nuts.

Bernard, Emile. Name of a famous chef de cuisine, born 1828, died 1897. Was chef for over 20 years to the Emperor William I. Co-author of "La Cuisine Classique," a famous standard work on cookery.

Besaigre, F. Sour, tart.

Besi, F. A variety of pear.

Bette, F. Mangel-wurzel.

Bette commune, F. White beet.

Betterave, F. Beetroot. (*See* BEETROOT.)

Beurre, F. (*See* BUTTER.)

Beurre manié. Butter and flour mixed together (in approx. equal proportions) used to thicken sauces.

Beurre noir (au), F. Anything done in butter which is cooked to a brownish black colour.

Beurre noisette, F. Nut-brown butter, E.—Butter melted over the fire until it begins to brown. *Beurre d'anchois*—anchovy butter. *Beurre frais*—fresh butter. *Beurre fondu*—melted butter. *Beurre salé*—salt butter. *Beurre (lait de)*—Buttermilk. *Beurrée*—Buttered or greased. *Beurré*—a kind of pear (butter-pear).

Biche, F. Hind Doe.

Bier, G. Beer.

Bière, F. Beer.

Bifsteck, G. Beefsteak.

Biftek, F. Name given on the Continent to fillet of beef rump steak or beefsteak.

Bigarade, F. Bitter or sour orange—Seville orange. It is also the name of an orange sauce; a *demi-glace* flavoured with the rind and juice of bitter oranges.

Bigarré, F. Varicoloured. Name of a French General.

Bigarreau, F. White-heart cherry.

Bigarrure, F. Is the name given to a rich stew made from pheasants, capons, etc. Literally, a variety of designs or colours. Insertions made in meat and filled with sliced meat of various kinds.

Bignon. A famous Parisian restaurateur.

Bilberry, Blaeberry. The best bilberries are found in the Scotch pine forests. In Germany, cold cooked bilberries are sometimes eaten at the commencement of dinner in place of soup. They are known, according to the locality, as Preissel-beeren and Heidelbeeren.

Bill of Fare. Menu, F. Literally, minute details, in a culinary sense; a list of dishes intended for a meal. Menu cards were first used at table in the year 1541.

Bind (To). To make a mixture and moisten it with egg, milk or cream, so that it will hold together and not curdle.

Bird's Nest (edible). Constructed by a small species of swallow, the Salangane, and found on the coast of China. There are two kinds, the black and white nests, the latter being much rarer and consequently more thought of than the former. The Chinese look upon these nests as a great delicacy, and make them into soup.

Biriani. An Indian dish made from lamb.

Bis (-e), F. Light brown.

Bis-blanc, F. Graham Wheat bread.

Biscaïen (-enne), F. Biscay Style.

Biscotin, F. A small, hard, sweet biscuit.

Biscottes, F. Thin slices of brioche paste, gently baked, buttered, and sugared, generally served with tea.

Biscuit, F. Literal meaning, twice baked. The term was originally applied to unfermented dough which had been twice baked in order to render it sufficiently dry to keep for a length of time. *Biscuits de Reims*—Savoy or finger biscuits. *Biscuit glacé*—glazed biscuit, ice cream biscuit.

Bishop. Drink made of wine, oranges and sugar. It was very popular in Germany during the Middle Ages.

Bisk. An ancient dish made of wild and tame birds, sweetbreads, cocks' combs, etc.

Bisque, F. Is the name given to certain soups usually made with shellfish.

Bisquotins, F. (*See* BISCOTIN.)

Bitter. An essence or liqueur made from different kinds of aromatic plants, herbs or fruits.

Bitter. F. Amer or amère.

Blackberry. Mûre de ronce, Baie de ronce, F.—Edible fruit of the bramble found growing wild in England. Very much esteemed by country people, and used for puddings, etc., as well as for jam and syrup.

Black Currant. Groseille noire, F. A small kind of grape fruit.

Black Grouse. Black game.

Black Jack. Name given to caramel, burnt sugar; sometimes used for colouring brown soups, brown sauces, and gravies.

Black Puddings. Boudin noir, F. Sausages made of pork, oatmeal, breadcrumbs, herbs, etc., enclosed in black skins. They are first boiled, and, when cold, either fried or toasted.

Blanc, F. A white broth or veal stock gravy.

Blanc tau), F. Cooked in white stock or served in white sauce.

Blanchaille, F. Whitebait, a delicate little fish usually fried in deep fat.

Blanching. The meat or vegetable is placed in boiling water for a short time, and then plunged into cold water. The object of blanching is to add firmness in order to facilitate the process of larding, or preserve the colour of white meats, vegetables, etc.

Blanchir, F. To blanch. To put anything on the fire in cold water until it boils; after which it is drained and plunged into cold water.

Blanc-mange, or **Blancmanger,** F. A white sweet food. A sweet cream set in a mould, made by boiling farinaceous substances in milk to the consistence of jelly. Originally a maigre soup, made of milk of almonds.

Blanquette, F. A stew usually made of veal or fowl, with a white sauce enriched with cream or egg-yolks. A white grape. A kind of pear.

Blé, F. Wheat, corn.

Blé turquois (Blé de Turquie), F. Maize. Indian corn.

Bleak. Brême, F. A small river fish with silvery scales.

Blette, F. Strawberry spinach.

Bleu (au), F. (*See* AU BLEU.)

Blinis. A kind of Russian pancake made with buck-wheat flour and served with caviare.

Bloaters. Are slightly salted and half-smoked dried herrings, which constitute a common breakfast dish in England. Those from Yarmouth are the best known; they are dried in smoke, whereas the bloaters cured in Norway are salted and dried, but not smoked.

Blond, F. Light coloured, fawn. *Blonde de Veau,* F.—A very rich veal broth, used for flavouring and enriching white soups and sauces.

Bloody Mary. A cocktail; 1 part vodka or aquavit to 2 parts tomato juice, seasoning and crushed ice.

22

Boar's Head. Hûre de sanglier, F. An historical Christmas dish in England. Moulds are used when they are manufactured commercially.

Bœuf, F. Beef. *Bœuf salé*—corned or salted beef.

Bœuf braisé, F. Braised beef.

Bœuf braisé Jardinière, F. Braised beef with mixed vegetables.

Bœuf en Daube, *f.* Spiced round of beef.

Bœuf en Persillade, F. Cold beef with parsley.

Bœuf fumé, F. Smoked beef.

Bohémien (-enne), (à la), F. Bohemian Style.

Boiling. Bouillir, F. A mode of cooking by moist heat, usually effected in water or stock.

Boisson, F. Drink.

Boistelle, F. When applied to fish dishes it denotes the inclusion of mushrooms.

Bolet, Boletus. A kind of mushroom.

Bologna Sausage. A large smoked sausage, made of bacon, veal, and pork suet; an Italian speciality principally manufactured at Bologna.

Bombay Duck. Also called Bummelo, Bumbalo or Bumalie fish, zoologists call it Harpodon. A fish found in the Indian waters. It is very nutritious, and possesses a peculiar yet delicate flavour. For exportation it is salted and cured, and is usually served with curry. In America and some parts of Europe it is considered a delicacy.

Bombe, F. An iced pudding lined with a rich custard and filled with fruit cream, shape of a bomb.

Bonbonnière, F. Bonbon box.

Bon-bons, F. Sugar confectionery; generally dainties for children.

Bon Chrétien. Name of a kind of winter-pear.

Bondon. A Neufchâtel cheese in the form of a bung. A stopper.

Bon Goût, F. Good taste. A much-used expression for highly flavoured dishes and sauces.

Bonne-bouche, F. Tit-bit. Name given to small savoury dishes, denoting the *hors d'œuvre* or savoury course.

Bonne Femme, F. Housewife. *A la bonne femme*—housewife style; name of a cream soup with herbs.

Bonnet de Turquie, F. A kind of ancient pastry made in moulds of the form of a Turkish bonnet.

Borage. Bourrache, F. An aromatic plant, excellent for

flavouring lettuce salads and iced drinks, claret cups, etc., sometimes called cucumber herb, on account of its flavour. The plant has spiny leaves and blue flowers.

Bord, Bordure. Border, edge.

Bordeaux, F. District in France which gives its name to the wine generally known in England as claret.

Bordelaise (à la), F. Name of a French sauce (brown), in which Bordeaux wine (claret) forms one of the ingredients. Also a garnish.

Borecole or **Scotch Kale.** A species of coarse, green, curly-leaved cabbage. (*See* KALE.)

Bortsch. A Polish soup in which beetroot forms the chief ingredient. Known as Bortsch Polonaise. There is also a Russian Bortsch which also includes beetroot.

Botte, F. Bunch, bundle.

Boucané (-e), F. Smoked.

Bouche, F. Mouth. *Bonne Bouche*—tit-bit; term frequently applied to small savouries and *hors d'œuvre* dishes.

Bouché, F. Corked, stopped up.

Bouchées, F. Small puff paste patties (petits *pates*), so as to be a traditional mouthful only. *Bouchées à la Reine,* F.— Small puff paste patties filled with chicken ragoût, invented by Marie Leczinska, wife of Louis XV.

Boucher (-ère), F. Butcher, Butcher's wife.

Bouchon, F. Cork.

Boucon, F. A kind of veal ragoût.

Boudin, F. A kind of small French sausage similar to black pudding, only much smaller.

Boudin blanc, F. White sausage.

Boudinade, F. A quarter of lamb stuffed with forcemeat.

Bouillant (-e), F. Boiling.

Bouille-à-baisse, F. A celebrated fish stew. A national French dish. Thackeray liked it so much that he wrote a ballad in its praise, beginning:

"This Bouille-a-baisse, a noble dish is,
   A sort of soup, a broth, or stew;
   A hotch-potch of all sorts of fishes,
      That Greenwich never could out-do," etc.

Bouilli, F. Boiled. Fresh boiled beef. A national French dish. *Bouilloire, Bouillote.* Boiler, kettle.

Bouillie, F. A drink of farina and milk.

Bouillon, F. A plain clear soup. Unclarified beef broth. Beef or veal broth. Nowadays the term also describes a powder or cube from which stock is made.

Boulanger, F. Baker.

Boule, F. Ball.

Boulettes, F. Little balls.

Bouquet garni, F. Bouquet of herbs. Faggot. A small bunch of savoury herbs, such as parsley, marjoram, chervil, tarragon, thyme, and bay-leaves. It is tied in a bunch to facilitate its removal after use. Used in stews, stocks, broths, braises, sauces, etc., to impart a rich flavour.

Bourbon. A whisky which is distilled from maize, especially popular in America.

Bourcette. Lamb's lettuce or corn salad. A pot herb.

Bourdalouse (à la) Bourdalou Style.

Bourgeoise (à la) F. A surname given to dishes, which signifies a dish prepared in a simple, homely but nevertheless tasty and wholesome, manner. It means a modest kind of home cookery.

Bourgogne, F. (Vin de Bourgogne.) Burgundy wine. Also the name of a rich brown sauce.

Bourgogne (à la), F. Burgundy style, name, and character given to dishes.

Bourguignote, F. A ragoût of truffles, usually served with game. *Bourguignonne (à la),* F.—Burgundy fashion, E.

Bourguinonne (à la), F. This surname is applied, as a general rule, to dishes, in the preparation of which Burgundy or Bordeaux wine and small braised button onions are introduced.

Bouride, F. A dish strongly flavoured with garlic.

Bourrache, F. Borage, E. Aromatic kitchen herb; also called cucumber herb, because it has the peculiar flavour of cucumbers.

Boutargue, F. (*See* POUTARGE.)

Bouteille, F. Bottle.

Brabançon (-onne) (à la), F. Brabant Style.

Brains. Cervelles. Calf's brain—*cervelle de veau.*

Braise, F. **Braising.** Meat cooked in a closely-covered stew-pan (braising pan or braisière) to prevent evaporation, so that the meat thus cooked retains not only its own juices, but also those of the articles added for flavouring, such as bacon, ham, soup vegetables, seasoning, etc., which are put with it. *Braisée,* or *Braiser,* F.—A mode of cooking known as braising, which is a combination of roasting and stewing. *Braisière, F.*—A large stewpan with ledges to the lid, used for braising meats, etc.

Brandade, F. Name given to a dish of stewed haddocks. A dish of cod *à la provençale,* with garlic, parsley, lemon juice and pepper, beaten up with olive oil.

Brander. Scotch name for the gridiron. Brandered steak: a grilled steak.

Brandy. Cognac, F. The name is derived from the German word *Branntwein* (literally translated, "burnt wine"). French brandy or Cognac, is most highly esteemed; Cognac (Department of Charente, France) is celebrated for the excellence of its brandy. (*See* also ARMAGNAC.) Brandy may be defined as an alcoholic liquor, the spirit of which is obtained by the distillation of wine from the grape.

Brasserie. A popular type of restaurant in Paris, Vienna, etc.

Brawn. Moulded cooked boar's or pig's head, etc.

Brazil Nuts. A hard nut contained in a three-sided shell.

Bread. Pain, F. Bread was probably invented either by the Egyptians or the Hebrews. The Greeks are said to have had more than fifty varieties of bread, and it was from them that the Romans learnt the art of making it. The use of yeast is of ancient date, but after the Roman era, leaven for a time banished yeast. It appears to have been again in use in England in 1634, and a little later the bakers in Paris began to use yeast imported from Flanders. For many centuries the use of fermented bread was confined to the upper classes, the bread of the peasantry consisting principally of the flat cakes which are still seen in remote parts of Norway and Sweden.

Breadcrumbs. Panure, F. To crumb. *Paner à la panure*—to coat with breadcrumbs. *Chaplure*—grated or pounded crust of browned bread.

Bread Fruit. The fruit of the bread-fruit tree (*arbre à pain*), F.), which is excellent as food.

Bread sauce. A sauce made from milk and breadcrumbs flavoured with onion. It is served with most roast poultry and game birds.

Breakfast. Déjeuner, F. The first meal of the day.

Break Flour (to). To stir gradually into the flour cold liquid until it becomes a smooth paste.

Bream. *Brême,* F.   A small species of river fish. Seasonable September to November.

Breast. Poitrine, F.   Part of an animal next below the neck.

Brésilien (-enne) (à la), F.   Brazilian Style.

Brésolle.   An entrée consisting of several kinds of meat. Also a ragoût of veal.

Breteuil (Baron de).   Name of a noted epicure of the reign of Louis XVI.

Bretonne (à la), F.   Brittany style; garniture, usually of haricot beans, whole or in purée.

Brider, F.   To truss poultry and game with a needle and thread.

Brie, F.   A soft cheese made in the Brie district of France.

Brié, F.   Kneaded paste for biscuits, etc.

Brier, F.   To beat or flatten paste with a rolling-pin.

Brife, F.   Large portion of bread.

Brifeur, F.   Gourmand.

Brignole, F.   A species of dark-red cooking plums from Brignoles, a district in France.

Brill, Barbue, F.   A flat fish of the turbot family, called in Scotland "Bonnet Fleuk," and in Devonshire and Cornwall "Kite" and "Bret."

Brillat-Savarin.   A noted writer on culinary matters; author of "La Physiologie du Goût," etc. Born 1755; died 1826.

Brin, F.   Sprig.

Brine. Marinade, F.   Used for the pickling and preservation of meat, fish, etc., and to impart certain aromatic flavours.

Brinjaul.   West Indian egg-plant, known in Bengal as Bangou, which name is supposed to come from the Portuguese "Bringella." (*See* AUBERGINE.)

Brioche, F.   A light French yeast cake, similar to Bath buns mixture, only much lighter. The favourite French breakfast bun, eaten hot with coffee or tea.

Brisket, Brisquet, F.   A brisket contains half the breast-bone with the commencement of the rib-bones attached on one side. The flesh consists of alternate layers of lean and fat. Generally applied to beef.

Brisotine, F.   Name of a light entrée of forcemeat, etc.

Brocard, F.   Young roebuck.

Broche, F.   French spit for roasting before an open fire.

Brochée, F.   Trussed and skewered ready for roasting.

Brochet, F.   Pike, Seasonable October to January. A fish to be found in almost all waters; much liked on account of its delicate flavour.

Brochette, F.   Skewer, spit.

Brocoli, F.   Broccoli. A hardy variety of the cauliflower; one variety is ready for use in the autumn, and the other in early spring.

Brödchen.   German for small dinner roll.

Broiling.   Ancient name for grilling. To cook over or in front of a fire by direct heat.

Brose.   A Scotch dish made by pouring boiling pot-liquor (or boiling water) on oatmeal or barley meal, with small pieces of fat meat.

Broth. Bouillon, F.   Beef stock or broth. An unclarified gravy soup, with or without garnish.

Brouet, F.   Broth, liquor. *Brouet d'andouille*—tripe liquor.

Brouillé, F.   Scrambled, mixed, beaten up; usually applied to eggs.

Broussin, F.   A mixture of soft cheese, pepper and vinegar.

Browning. Caramel, F.   Liquid colouring matter made in the form of thick syrup by browning sugar to nearly burning point.

Broyée, F.   Crushed or coarsely ground.

Brugnon, F.   Velvet skin peach.

Brûlant, F.   Burning, alight, burning hot.

Brûlée, F.   Burnt.

Brun, F.   Brown. *Brunâtre*—brownish.

Brunoise, F.   A class of French clear or thick soups, with finely-cut vegetable garnish. Brunoy is a district in France (*Seine-et-Oise*), celebrated for the growth of fine spring vegetables.

Brussels Sprouts. Choux de Bruxelles, F.   A kind of small cabbage seasonable from November to March.

Brut, F.   Unsweetened, natural, raw.

Bruxellois (-e) à la), F.   Brussels Style.

Bruyère (Coq de).   Heath cock.

Bucarde, Boucarde, Bucardier.   (*See* COCKLE.)

Bubble and Squeak.   A well-known old English dish, made with boiled and minced cabbage and potatoes, and originally slices of cold meat, fried together.

Buck Rarebit.   A Welsh rarebit with the addition of a poached egg placed on the top of the cheese.

Buckwheat, Sarrasin, F.   A species of Polygonum grown in

Germany, Brittany, etc., for feeding horses, cattle, and poultry. In America buck-wheat cakes are a common article of diet.

Buffet, F.   A place for refreshments; a sideboard.

Buisson, F.   A cluster or a bunch of shrimps, crayfish, or lobster; also applied to a method of twisting up pastry to a point. A method of cutting fillets of sole for deep-frying *filets de sole frits en buisson.*

Bullace.   The bullace-tree is a native of warm countries, but is now cultivated also in more northern regions; its fruit is a kind of plum, and very much like the damson. The bullace, however, has not the pleasant roughness of taste so characteristic of the damson; moreover, it is round in form while the damson is oval.

Biltong.   Dried antelope meat. Dried beef.

Bumbo.   A kind of punch, made of spirits, etc. An American drink.

Bummalo.   (*See* BOMBAY DUCK.)

Bunion.   Earth nut. Also name of a kind of cheap almond imported from Italy.

Buns.   A well-known kind of light and spongy tea-cakes. The special buns for Good Friday—"hot-cross buns"— flavoured with cinnamon, and marked with a $+$, are particularly familiar to English people.

Burbot.   Eel-pout. (*See* BARBOTTES and LOTTE, F.)

Burdwan.   A savoury dish made of re-heated poultry, venison, or meat; of Indian origin.

Burgall.   The American blue perch.

Burgundy.   (*See* BOURGOGNE, F.)

Burnt-sugar Colouring.   (*See* CARAMEL, F.)

Burst Rice.   Is to put it to boil in cold water; when boiling, the grains of rice will burst.

Bustard.   A large game-bird.

Butter.   Beurre, F.   To butter moulds—*beurrer les moules. Sauté au beurre*—done in butter (tossed). Butter was first used as a food by the Hebrews; the early Greeks and Romans used it as a medicine or ointment. Butter was discovered at a very early period, and in the first century of the present era Pliny mentions it in terms which imply that it was an article of everyday use.

Butter-bean.   A variety of Lima bean.

Butterfly shrimps or prawns.   Prawns or shrimps which have been shelled and slit down the back, into which strips of bacon are inserted. They are then floured and fried in oil. A suitable sauce is served with them, e.g., devilled sauce or Chinese barbecue sauce.

Butter-milk. Babeurre, F. That portion of the cream which is left after the butter has been made from it.

Buttery. A place for keeping butts; has no connection with the word "butter."

Buvette, F. Coffee-house, bar, or refreshment-room.

Cabaret, F. An inn.

Cabaretier (-ière), F. Innkeeper.

Cabbage. (Chou or Choux, F.). A well-known vegetable plant of several species forming a head in growing. Originally it was the wild-growing colewort, still to be found on the cliffs of our sea coast. In its cultivated state it was first brought into this country from Holland, about the time of Henry VIII., when the cultivation of vegetables was here hardly known.

Cabillaud, F. Codfish. A sea fish, in season from September till end of April; obtainable all the year. The oil from the liver of the cod is highly beneficial for lung and chest complaints. *Cabillaud farci*—stuffed codfish.

Cabus, F. Broccoli.

Cacao, F. Cocoa.

Cachiment, F. Popular name for the tree *Anone, F.*, which produces the *pomme cannelle* or custard apple (*q.v.*).

Caen, F. A town of France famous for its tripe and other delicacies (*à la mode de Caen*).

Café, F. Coffee (*q.v.*). A coffee-house or restaurant. A beverage prepared from the coffee berries after they have been roasted and ground. *Café au lait,*—coffee with milk. *Café double*—black coffee of double strength. *Café noir*—black coffee. *Café turc*—Turkish coffee. *Café frappé*—iced coffee. *Café vièrge*—an infusion of the whole coffee beans. *Caffeine*—a bitter substance obtained from coffee. *Cafétière*—coffee-pot.

Caille, F. (*See* QUAIL.) *Cailles farcies*—stuffed quails. *Cailles rôties,* F.—roast quails. Quails are rarely caught in their wild state in the British Isles. They are imported from France but are also available all the year round from farms in this country.

Caillebotte, F. Curds.

Cailleteau, F. Young quail.

Caillot-rosat, F. A kind of pear with a rose flavour.

Caisse, F. Case (ramaquin case), etc.

Cake. Gâteau, F. Generally a mixture of flour, dried fruits, etc., with butter, eggs, or B.P., used to make it light, baked in tins or small patty-pans.

Calf. Veal. Veau, F.

Calf's Brains. Cervelles de veau, F. Calf's ears—*oreilles de veau,* F. Calf's feet—*pieds de veau,* F. A good jelly can be obtained from these by boiling. Calf's head—*tête de veau,* F. Calf's kidney—*rognons de veau,* F. Calf's liver—*foie de veau,* F.—Calf's sweetbreads—*ris de veau,* F. Calf's tongue—*langue de veau,* F. Calf's tail soup—*consommé queue de veau*; *potage queue de veau.*

Calipash. A portion of glutinous meat to be found in the upper shell of the turtle.

Calipee. The glutinous meat found in the under part of a turtle's under shell.

Calvilles, F. A kind of French apple.

Camarine, F. Crowberry, crakeberry.

Camembert, F. Cheese made in the district of that name in France.

Canapé, F. Much used for *hors d'œuvre* and savoury dishes. The word means sofa; it consists, as a rule, of slices of bread cut into various sizes, used plain, or fried in oil or butter, or toasted.

Canard, F. Duck. *Canard rôti*—roast duck. *Canard sauvage*—wild duck. *Canard des bois*—wood duck.

Canary Wines. Produced in the Canary Islands; many of them resemble Madeira.

Cancale. A place in France famous for its oysters.

Candied Peel. Consists of the outer rind of lemon, orange, citron, or lime, encrusted with sugar, and is used as an ingredient of minced meat for mince pies and various sorts of cake.

Cane, F. Hen duck.

Caneton, F. Duckling. *Caneton rôti,* F.—Roast duckling. *Caneton de Rouen,* F.—Rouen duckling. Rouen is celebrated for the superiority of its ducklings; they do not bleed them as here, but thrust a skewer through the brain, thus keeping the blood in the flesh.

Canneberge, F. Cranberry (which see).

Cannelons, F., or **Canelons.** Small rolls of puff pastry filled with savoury mince meat, fish, poultry or game.

Cantaloup, F. *Hors d'œuvre* of iced Roche (Rock) melon. Iced fruit; usually a Roche melon or bananas served at the beginning of luncheon or dinner.

Cantharelle, F. (*See* CHANTERELLE.)

Canvas Back Duck is a native of North America, where it owes its popular name to the wavy lines and speckles on its otherwise white feathers. They are more difficult to obtain than other ducks, being excellent divers and strong on the wing. It is held in high esteem in the United States.

Capelan, F. A delicately flavoured fish of the cod family, resembling smelt.

Capendu, F. Red apple.

Capercailzie. This bird is a member of the grouse family, and possesses a peculiar flavour. It is usually cooked and served like grouse. The capercailzie is the largest of the gallinaceous birds of Europe, and is about the size of a small turkey. It is generally to be found in the north of Europe, particularly Northern Scotland. The hen bird which is mottled in colour is much smaller than the male.

Caper. Câpre, F. The unopened flower-buds of a plant which grows wild among the rocks of Greece and Northern Africa, and now cultivated in the south of Europe. They are imported from Italy, Sicily, and the south of France, after being first pickled in salt and vinegar.

Caperon, F. Hautboy, a large white strawberry.

Capillaire. A kind of fern. A syrup flavoured with orange-flowers, etc.—*sirop de capillaire.*

Capilotade. A culinary expression for a mixed hash.

Caplan. (*See* CAPELAN.)

Caplin. A small fish of delicate flavour, resembling smelts.

Capon. Chapon, F. The capon is the common cock-bird,

treated with hormones to develop its growth. Weight 6–9 lbs.

Capron. (*See* CAPERON.)

Capsicum. The capsicum produces the condiment known as red or cayenne pepper. There are various species of capsicum; the fruit is extremely pungent and stimulating, and is employed in sauces, mixed pickles, etc.

Capucin (Barbe de), F. (*See* CHICORY.)

Capucine, F. Indian cress. Nasturtium.

Carafe, F. Decanter.

Caramel, F. Name of a favourite sweetmeat. Liquid colouring matter, made by browning sugar to nearly burning-point. Commonly known as "Black Jack." Also used for coating moulds for crème caramel, in which case the sugar is cooked to amber colour.

Carapace, F. Shell.

Caraway. Cumin, F. The seeds are the dried fruit of the plant on which they grow. In Germany they are used for sweet as well as savoury dishes. This plant has long been valued and cultivated in Europe for the sake of its well-known aromatic seeds, which are, however, strictly not seeds, but the *pericarps* into which the fruit in this order splits when ripening. They are largely employed in pharmacy as an aromatic stimulant and flavouring ingredient, but their chief use is as a spice by bakers, confectioners and cooks. Much eaten in Scotland, when sugared, and known as "carvies," *anglicé* caraway "comfits."

Carbonade, F. Stewed or braised meat, usually cooked in beer.

Carbonado. An ancient dish prepared from a fowl or joint of veal or mutton, roasted, carved, and cut across and across. The pieces were then basted with butter, sprinkled with breadcrumbs, and grilled.

Carcasse, F. Carcase. The body of an animal; the bones or skeleton of poultry or game. (U.S. Carcass.)

Cardamine, F. Wild cress, or bitter cress.

Cardamom. Cardamome, F. Known as the "Seed of Paradise," a stimulant aromatic spice. The seeds of a plant of the ginger family, which grows abundantly in the mountain forests of the coast of Malabar. They are used largely in India and Ceylon in cookery, flavouring, etc.; also in curries, cakes and confectionery. In Northern Europe, as a spice for flavouring cakes, and in the preparation of liqueurs.

Medicinally it is one of the best stimulant aromatics. An antiseptic of the highest value.

Carde, F. The edible portion of the cardoon. Mostly served braised or else as a purée.

Carde à la Moëlle, F. Pieces of marrow braised with bacon.

Cardinal (à la). Applies to a garnish for fish dishes consisting of slices of lobster and truffles. Also the name of a sauce, prepared from lobsters, béchamel, fish stock and truffle essence.

Cardon, F. Cardoon. A garden plant resembling artichokes in flavour. The stalks of the inner leaves bleached till white are crisp and tender. Used like celery in stews, soups and salads.

Carelet. (*See* CARRELET), F.

Carême, F. Lent.

Carême (A.). The name of a celebrated chef, born in Paris in 1784, died 1833; author of several culinary works, chef to the Prince Regent, George IV. of England, and the Emperor Alexander I. of Russia. Many dishes are named after him.

Caret, F. Green turtle.

Carmine. Carmin, F. Crimson. Red colouring used in confectionery, etc.

Carotte, F. Carrot. A garden plant in its root (red or yellow-coloured). Carrots were first introduced into England by Flemish gardeners in the time of Elizabeth I; in the reign of James I. they were still so uncommon that ladies wore bunches of them on their hats and on their sleeves instead of feathers.

Carousel. The name of a revolving service counter used in industrial catering establishments.

Carp, Carpe, F. A fresh-water fish.

Carpeau, F. Small carp.

Carpentras (à la). A surname to dishes flavoured with, or consisting of, truffles as a garnish. Carpentras, like Perigord, is a district where truffles of excellent flavour and size grow largely.

Carré, F. Neck. The rib part of veal, mutton, lamb or pork.

Carrelet, F. Flounder. A small flat fish, in season all the year except in May, June, and July.

Carte du Jour (la), F. The bill of fare for the day; a list of daily dishes with the prices attached to each dish.

Cartouche, F.   Cartridge. A culinary term meaning a circular piece of greased paper, used for covering meat, etc., during the process of cooking.

Carvie.   Caraway seed. (*See* CARAWAY.)

Carviol.   A vegetable very much the same as cauliflower, best known and cultivated in Austria.

Casanova (Cazanova).   Name of a salad composed of celery and truffles.

Case.   Caisse, F.

Caseine.   The coagulated flesh-forming substance of milk and certain leguminous plants. The curd of milk from which cheese is produced. Cheese is therefore an important flesh-forming food in a concentrated form.

Casha.   An Indian dish, a kind of cream flavoured with mace.

Cashew Nut.   A nut grown in the West Indies and South America.

Cassareep.   The prepared juice of the cassava. The basis of many sauces and of the West Indian pepper-pot.

Cassava.   The refined starch of the manioc; when further refined, cassava is known as tapioca.

Casse, F.   Case, pan (*casse à roti*—dripping pan).

Casserole, F.   A copper stewpan, also a fireproof earthenware or glass pan. When used in menus it sometimes indicates a shape of rice, baked paste crust, filled with minced meat, game purée, etc., etc. (*See* also POULET EN CASSEROLE.)

Cassia.   A name given by the ancients to a kind of aromatic bark. It is referred to in the Scriptures and by classical writers. This spice, also called cascarilla, is essentially a cheaper and coarser kind of cinnamon, for which it forms a fair substitute, its essential oil being chemically similar, although inferior in fragrance and flavour.

Cassis, F.   The part which is attached to the tail end of a loin of veal; also black-currant syrup or liqueur.

Cassolette, F.   Small casserole shapes, to hold one portion.

Casson, F.   Broken loaf sugar; broken cocoa-nibs.

Cassonade, F.   Moist brown sugar. Sugar which has not been highly refined.

Cassoulette, F.   Variety of delicate stew.

Castelane, F.   A kind of green plum, similar to the greengage.

Catfish.   A fish of the shark family.

Catsup. (*See* KETCHUP.)

Caul. Crépine, F. A membrane in the shape of a net covering the lower portion of a pig's bowels, used for wrapping up minced meat, sausages, salpicon, etc.

Cauliflower. Chou-fleur, F. A delicate and highly prized vegetable of the cabbage family.

Caviar, F. Caviare. The salted roe of sturgeon or sterlet (fish eggs). Caviare contains twice the nutriment of almost all meats, and is almost equal to pork, which contains the highest amount of nutritive elements of any meat. The sterlet is a species of sturgeon not more than two or three feet in length, but possessing very large ova.

Cayenne Pepper. (*See* PEPPER.)

Cédrat, F. A kind of citron-tree; its fruit is used for cakes, puddings, and ice-creams, and a special kind of oil is also prepared from this fruit.

Celeriac or **Celery Root.** Céléri rave, F. A turnip-rooted celery, of which the root only is used; usually served as a vegetable, stewed in broth or served with melted butter.

Celery. Céleri, F. A salad plant, eaten raw or dressed as salad. Cooked, it is served in various ways as a vegetable or in soups.

Célestin. A monk so named after Pope Célestin. *à la Celéstine*, F., from the Latin *cœlestis* (heavenly). Several dishes are called after this name.

Celsius. The degree Celsius is a degree of temperature. The Celsius scale is the same as Centigrade scale but as the term "centigrade" is already used in France with another meaning (0.0001 of a right angle), Celsius will probably be adopted to avoid confusion when Britain goes "metric".

Cendre (la), F. Ashes or embers. *Cuit sous la cendre*—cooked under the ashes.

Cèpe or **Ceps,** F. Esculent boletus, an edible mushroom of yellowish colour, having an agreeable and nutty flavour, largely cultivated in the Bordeaux district.

Cercelle. (*See* SARCELLE), F.

Cerf, F. Deer, stag, hart. The meat of venison.

Cerfeuil, F. (*See* CHERVIL.)

Cerise, F. Cherry. A small stone fruit of many varieties. Cherries were known in Asia as far back as the 14th century. Pliny states that Lucullus first brought this fruit to Italy about seventy years before the Christian Era, and records that the

36

Romans afterwards introduced the cherry-tree into Great Britain. The name is derived from Kerasos (Cerasus), a town in Asia Minor.

Cerneau, F. The kernel of a green walnut. Usually prepared in salt-water. A red wine is also made from these kernels, called vin de cerneaux, which is to be drunk in the walnut season.

Cerneaux Confits, F. Preserved green walnuts.

Cervelas, F. A kind of a thick and short smoked sausage made of pork, and seasoned with salt, pepper, and spices.

Cervelle, F. Brain. A substance within the skull of an animal. Veal, lamb, pork, and beef brains are used in cookery.

Chablis. A famous French white Burgundy wine, grown in and near Chablis, in the Burgundy district.

Chair, F. Flesh. *Chair blanche*—white meat. *Chair noire*—dark meat. *Chair à saucisse*—suasage meat.

Chambord (à la). Method of cooking fish (particularly carp) in a *court-bouillon au vin blanc* which is subsequently reduced to a white sauce with quenelles, white champignons, *rognons de coq,* etc. Named after the locality of Chambord or the duc de Chambord.

Champagne, F. Sparkling wine of the Champagne district, which includes Reims, Epernay and Chalons-sur-Marne. The region produces wines which differ in every vineyard, and the most appreciated champagnes are composed of skilful blends of more than one kind of wine. The renown of champagne as a sparkling wine only dates from the 17th century. The term *fine champagne* is applied to old cognac or brandy of fine quality, produced in the Charente district.

Champignons, F. Mushrooms. A fungus. *Champignon de prairie,* F.—Field mushroom.

Chancelier (à la), F. Chancellor.

Chanterelle or **Cantharelle,** F. A species of mushroom.

Chantilly (à la), F. Chantilly Style, usually with whipped cream.

Chapelure, F. Rasped crust of bread.

Chapon, F. (*See* CAPON). Also a piece of bread boiled in soups; a crust of bread rubbed with garlic.

Chaponneau, F. Young capon.

Char. A fresh-water fish, mostly found in the English Lake district. It belongs to the same family as the salmon and trout, and has the same pink and oily flesh.

Charbonnée, F. Burnt.

Charcuterie, F. The word means badly carved; but in a culinary sense it denotes pork, prepared in any fashion. Black pudding, pig's feet truffled, smoked pig's ear with truffles, Nancy sausages, saveloy, pig's liver, are all items of charcuterie. *Charcutier, F.* (from chair-cuite)—a purveyor of cooked and dressed meats.

Charente or Charentais, F. A variety of melon originally from the Charente district of France but now also grown in other countries notably Israel. It is a small choice melon, half of which is usually a portion; cointreau or similar liqueur is often served in the centre.

Charlotte, F. A corruption of the old English word Charlyt, which means a dish of custard. *Charlotte Russe*—Russian Charlotte, a cream encrusted with thin biscuits. *Charlotte de Pomme*—Apple Charlotte, consists of thin slices of bread, steeped in clarified butter ranged in symmetrical order in plain moulds and filled with apple purée, and baked.

Charponnière, F. Name of a special kind of stew-pan.

Chartreuse, F. Carthusian originally meant various kinds of vegetables or fruit, dished up in the shape of goblets set in aspic or jelly. In its degenerate form, cooked game, small poultry, etc., are cooked and dressed in Chartreuse style, either hot or cold. In modern cookery also applied to fruit macédoine in jelly shape with cream in centre. Also name of a delicious and rather costly liqueur of a green or yellow colour. First distilled by the monks of Grande Chartreuse, near Grenoble, France.

Chasselas. A kind of white grape, used for wine-making.

Chasseur, F. A term signifing hunter's style or dishes which may be cooked quickly. Dishes with this name are characterized by *Sauce Chasseur.*

Châtaigne, F. Chestnut, E. Used for stuffing and sweet dishes. (*See* CHESTNUT.)

Châteaubriand. Name of Viscount Francois Auguste, a great French gourmand, born in 1769, died 1848. A favourite dish of double fillet steak is called after him.

Chaud (-e), F. Warm.

Chaudeau, F. A sweet sauce served with puddings, etc.

Chaudfroid, or Chaud-froid, F. Name given to dishes such as chicken, game, cutlets, etc., masked with cold sauce and

38

served cold, usually garnished with savoury jelly and truffles.

Chaufferette, F. Chafing dish.

Chaussons, F. French round, flat, light pasties sometimes filled with jam.

Cheese. Fromage, F. The curd of milk coagulated and pressed. As a food it possesses very distinct nutritive properties. Its principal element is caseine, which is the chemical equivalent of the white of egg, gluten of wheat, and the fibrin of meat. Cheese, although nutritious, needs to be cooked over very gentle heat to make it easily digestible in the mass.

Cheesecake. Talmouse, F. A pastry; tartlets made of a very light and flaky crust, with a mixture of cheese-curd, or almond, etc., in the centre.

Chef-de-Cuisine, F. Chief of the kitchen; head cook.

Chemise, F. Robe, jacket (of potato). *Chemisé*—lined (a mould coated with jelly, forcemeat, or paste).

Cherry. Cerise, F. The fruit of the cherry-tree. Some 300 different varieties of this fruit are now known, of which the black of Morella (*guigne*) is the best for cooking purposes. The white-heart cherry (*Bigarreau*) is the best of dessert cherries. (*See also* CERISE.)

Chervil. Cerfeuil, F. An aromatic plant, the leaves of which are used to flavour salads, sauces, soups, etc. The flavour resembles both parsley and fennel. The leaves are also used for decorating moulds. The root is poisonous.

Chestnut. Marron or Châtaigne, F. Named after the town of Castanea in Thessaly. A nutritious and easily-digestible fruit; used as stuffing for turkeys, poulards, and capons; also as an ingredient in soups, sauces, and purées. As a sweet or dessert it is also used in various ways. Chestnuts were a favourite food among the ancient Greeks.

Chevalier (à la), F. Chevalier Style.

Chevesne, Chevaine or **Chevenne, F.** (*See* CHUB.)

Cheveuse d'Ange, F. A sweetmeat prepared from young carrots. It is also the name of a very fine type of vermicelli.

Chevreuil, F. Roe-buck, roe-deer, E.

Chevreuse, F. Small goose-liver tartlet; a distinguished statesman of the latter part of the 17th century—Claude de Lorraine, duc de Chevreuse, after whom certain dishes are named.

Chiche, F. Chick peas.

Chicken Broth. Usually made by simmering an old hen until all the goodness is extracted. A little vegetable and pearl-barley is sometimes added.

Chicken. Poulet or Volaille, F. Chic or squab chickens—*poussins, F.*

Chicken in the basket. A term used to describe small pieces of chicken (drumsticks or small wings etc.) which have been coated with breadcrumbs or batter and deep-fried.

Chicken turbot. (*See* TURBOT.)

Chicorée, F. Chicory, also called succory and endive. The young root is used as a vegetable, and the leaves as a salad. The roots are transplanted to a dark place for bleaching, and the fresh growth of leaves produces the well-known Barbe de Capucin, a salad much used in France. The mature root roasted and ground produces the chicory used to adulterate coffee. Chicory is found growing wild on the borders of our cornfields, but the plant is cultivated in all parts of Europe.

Chiffonnade, F. Herb leaves, finely shredded.

Chine of Pork. The chine, when cut from a small pig, consists of two undivided loins, and corresponds to a saddle of mutton. In a large pig, whose sides are intended for bacon, the name is given to the spine or backbone, and the meat attached, the amount of which varies considerably according to locality.

Chinese Artichoke. (*Stachys Tuberifera.*) The roots present a spiral appearance, are pearly white, and eaten raw they are intermediate in flavour between a succulent radish and a Jerusalem artichoke. When cooked and served with melted butter, in much the same manner as the globe artichoke, they are delicious in flavour.

Chinois, F. A pointed strainer with very fine holes, used for straining soups, sauces, and gravies. A Chinese fruit like a small tangerine orange, generally sold in crystallised form.

Chipolata. Small Italian sausages. Originally an Italian ragoût. This name is also given to dishes which contain an addition of Italian sausages or a kind of mixed minced meat with which they are served.

Chitterlings. The boiled intestine or gut of ox, also of calf and pig; and small tripe. The name is also applied to sausage.

Chive. Ciboulette, F. A small green perennial onion, chiefly used in salads and soups.

Chocolate. Chocolat, F. The beans of the Theobroma cacao tree, manufactured and made into paste, cake, or powder. The tree is a native of the West Indies and South America. The cocoa (or cacao) bean was held as a symbol of hospitality by the Siamese. In olden times it served as a current coin in Yucatan. Chocolate has been known as a favourite beverage for more than 400 years. Introduced into England in 1520 from Mexico, and sold in London coffee-houses in 1650.

Choisi (-e), F. Choice.

Chopine, F. Half-bottle.

Chop Suey. (Chinese). A type of stew which may consist of rice, noodles, bean sprouts, bamboo shoots and mushrooms. It is then finished with the ingredient from which it takes its name, e.g., Chicken or Lobster, etc.

Chota Hazri. The first (or little) breakfast, in India.

Chou, F. Cabbage. Chou blanc, F.; white cabbage, E. Chou vert, F.; green cabbage, E. Chou rouge, F.; red cabbage, E. Chou farci, F.; stuffed cabbage, E. Chou de Bruxelles, F.; Brussels sprouts, E.

Choucroute, F. Sauerkraut, E. A kind of pickled cabbage.

Chou-fleur, F. (*See* CAULIFLOWER.)

Chou-rave, F. (*See* KOHL-RABI.)

Choux-au-lard, F. Cabbage and bacon.

Chow-chow. Name of a kind of pickle consisting of a combination of various vegetables, such as cauliflower buds, button onions, gherkins, French beans, and tiny carrots. These are preserved in a kind of mustard sauce, seasoned with strongly-flavoured aromatic spices.

Chowder. A dish of American origin. It consists of boiled pickled pork cut in slices, fried onions, slices of turbot or other fish, and mashed potatoes, all placed alternately in a stewpan, seasoned with spices and herbs, claret and ketchup, and simmered. Also made with clam (clam chowder).

Chrysanthemum. Its taste is somewhat similar to that of cauliflower, only more delicate. If shredded finely and mixed with a salad cream, it makes a most delicious salad. In Japan these edible flowers are a common article of diet, being abundantly displayed in grocers' shops during November and December. They are eaten as a salad, and almost every variety may be used, but those of a deep yellow are esteemed best for the purpose. The taste for them is, no doubt, an acquired one, as it is for most things.

Chub. Chevesne, F. A fresh-water fish, resembling the carp. Very little used for cooking purposes, it being exceedingly bony.

Chutney. An Indian condiment made of a variety of fruits, sugar, spices, and vinegar.

Ciboule, Ciboulette, F. (*See* CHIVE.)

Cider. Cidre, F. The juice of apples fermented and used as a drink, principally in the country. Cider is also largely made in France and Germany.

Cimier, F. Saddle, haunch (generally used of venison).

Cinnamon. Cannelle, F. The inner bark of a species of laurel. This shrub grows wild in Indonesia and Ceylon, but is cultivated in the East and West Indies. Cinnamon has been in use from the remotest antiquity, is mentioned in the Old Testament by a name which is derived from the Hebrew *qinnàmon*=a reed or cane, almost the same as that which it still bears in most languages.

Ciseer, F. To make incision in the under-skin of a fish so that when grilled it may not crack.

Citric Acid. This acid is used in small quantities for boiled sugar goods; it imparts body, and prevents the sugar from getting moist. It is obtained from the lemon and lime, but is also obtained from other acid fruits, such as sour cherries, Seville oranges, raspberries, currants, etc. Commercially it is obtainable in clear crystals or white powder.

Citron, F. Lemon. The fruit of the lemon-tree (citronier, F.), or citrus limonum; a native of the North-West Indian Provinces. This fruit had been introduced by the Arabs into Spain, whence it was spread over Europe, and is now cultivated in almost all the tropical and sub-tropical countries. An important culinary condiment. *Citronnat*, F.—Candied lemon-peel; the preserved peel of lemon. *Citronné*, F.—Anything which has the taste or flavour of lemon.

Citronnelle, F. Balm mint.

Citrouille, F. A kind of vegetable-marrow or pumpkin.

Civet or **Civette,** F. A brown stew of hare, venison, or other game.

Clam. Lucene, F. A large bivalvular shellfish highly prized in the United States. (*See* CHOWDER.)

Claret. The English name for Bordeaux wines, derived from the French *clairet*. The term originated in Scotland, where Bordeaux wines were largely consumed until the union with

42

England, when a preferential tariff led to the exclusion of French wines in favour of port.

Clarification. An operation which is so termed when any liquid is clarified. For the clarification of stock for consommés and savoury jellies, finely minced raw meat, eggs, and water are used; whilst for sweet jellies, whites of egg and lemon juice are used for a similar purpose, *Clarifié*—clarified, filtered. *Clarify*—to render clear. Lean beef is generally used to clear stock, and whites of eggs to clarify jelly.

Clear Soup. (*See* CONSOMMÉ, F.) Clarified stock, being a strong broth obtained by boiling meat, bones and vegetables.

Cloche, F. A glass utensil used to cover certain items whilst they are cooking, e.g.: mushrooms—*Champignons Sous Cloche*. Also the name of a cover used to keep food warm or to protect foodstuffs on service counters.

Clou de Girofle, F. (*See* CLOVE.)

Clouté, F. Studded. To insert nail-shaped pieces of truffle, bacon, or tongue, into fowl, poulards, cushions of veal, and sweetbreads. The holes to receive them are made by means of a skewer. (*See also* CONTISER.)

Clove. Girofle, F. An aromatic spice. The plant (a tree) is indigenous to the Molucca Islands; generally used for flavouring soups, stocks, meats, ragoûts, and sweets. The Dutch make a delicious marmalade from green cloves. Cloves are the unopened flower buds of a small evergreen shrub resembling the bay or laurel, which is much cultivated in tropical regions of America. The buds are gathered while still green, smoked by wood fire and then dried in the sun.

Clupe, F. A genus of fishes, of which the herring is the type, and which includes the sardine, anchovy, brisling, pilchard, shad, etc.

Coca. Kola or Koka. The nut of *Erythroxylon coca*. A stimulating narcotic; a tonic and restorative; taken alone with or after food.

Cochineal. Cochenille, F. A deep red liquid colouring substance used for colouring creams, jellies, icing, etc. It is obtained from insects known as coccus, indigenous to Mexico and Guatemala. The insects are dried in an oven heated to 150 degrees Fahrenheit. It requires 70,000 insects to produce a pound of dye.

Cochon de Lait, F. Sucking-pig.

Cochonnaille, F. Hog's or pig's pudding.

Cock Ale. An ancient dish, made of ale, minced meat of a boiled cock, and other ingredients.

Cock-a-leekie. A soup made of leeks and fowls; a favourite Scotch dish.

Cock Turkey. Dindon, F. (*See also* TURKEY.)

Cockle. Name of a nutritious shellfish, generally found on the seashore. The largest cockles come from the Scilly Islands, the North Devonshire coast and the Hebrides.

Cocks' Combs. Crêtes de coq, F. Used when cooked for garnishing rich ragoûts.

Coco. (*See* COCONUT.) *Coco* is Spanish for bogie, and it is said the coconut was thus named for its resemblance to a distorted human face.

Cocoa. A beverage prepared from seeds of the Theobroma Cacao tree. (*See also* CHOCOLATE.)

Coconut. The fruit of a palm which grows abundantly in the East Indies. From the fibre of the outer husk matting is made. The nut is grated and added to curries, pastry, and confectionery. Desiccated coconut is a useful preparation.

Cocotte, F. Small earthenware fireproof pans, in single portion size or larger; cooking vessel. As *cocotte de volaille*: *poulet en cocotte*: *œufs en cocotte,* etc.

Cod. Cabillaud, F. A sea-fish. The cod grows to a large size, weighing from 14 to 40 lbs.

Codlin. Name of an excellent kind of cooking apple.

Codling. Moruau, F. A young cod.

Cod Sounds. Nau de morue, F. The sounds (air bladders) are removed as soon as the fish are caught, and are salted and packed in barrels. They are usually either broiled or stewed in milk.

Coffee. (*See* CAFÉ, F.) The berry of a shrub; a beverage made from the berries when roasted and ground. Originally grown in Arabia; now cultivated in all tropical countries. Fine varieties come from Jamaica, Java and Mysore.

Cognac. (*See* BRANDY.)

Coing, F. Quince. A fruit used for compôte and marmalade.

Coinguarde, F. A liqueur distilled from quinces. Also name of marmalade made from quinces and grape fruit.

Colbert, F. A French clear soup and other dishes named after Jean Baptiste Colbert, a statesman in the reign of Louis XIV. of France, 1619–1683.

Colcannon. A vegetable pie—*i.e.,* mashed potatoes and

boiled cabbage, previously fried in butter or dripping and baked. Originally a Scotch dish, corrupted from Kailcannon.

Cole Slaw. A salad made of finely shredded raw cabbage, carrots and onions mixed with mayonnaise.

Colewort. A variety of cabbage, originally the name of the wild plant from which all the cultivated varieties of cabbage are derived.

Colin, F. A species of cod considered somewhat inferior. The small fish are sometimes known as pollock whiting. In France the name *Colin* is given to hake.

Collared. Meat pickled, tightly rolled boiled with herbs and spices, and pressed to shape until cold.

Collet, F. Scrag-end of the neck of mutton or veal.

Collops. Escalopes, F. Properly applied to any small boneless piece of meat but often used, instead of the full term "minced collops," to denote minced savoury meat, generally beef or mutton.

Colombe, F. Pigeon, dove.

Coloquinte, F. Colocynth, a bitter cucumber.

Colouring. A thick syrup made of loaf sugar, fresh butter and à little water, simmered in a sugar boiler over a gentle heat till it is a bright brown colour.

Colza. A varity of cabbage from which a burning oil is extracted.

Compiègne, F. A light yeast cake with crystallised fruit. Also the name of the French castle built by Louis XIV. of France.

Compote, F. Fruits stewed in syrup, also a brown stew of small birds.

Compote de Pigeon, F. Pigeon stew.

Concasser, F. To pound or chop, coarsely.

Concombre, F. (*See* CUCUMBER.)

Condé. Name of an old French family; Prince Louis de Condé (1621–1686) was a famous field-marshal. Several soups and sweets, of which rice forms an essential part, are styled "à la Condé."

Condiments. Highly-flavoured seasoning, spices, etc.

Confit, F. Comfit. Preserved in sugar. *Confiture,* F.—Fruit jams. Also sweetmeats of sugar and fruits. Fruit pastes, etc.

Conger Eel. Congre, F. The conger lives in the seas, and does not enter fresh-water streams like other eels. It often grows to a length of eight feet. This fish is less oily than eel.

45

Consommé, F. Clear soup. The clarified liquor in which meat or poultry has been boiled, or the liquor from the stock-pot clarified, with or without meat and soup vegetables.

Contiser, F. To insert small strips or pieces of truffle, ham, bacon, etc., into fillets of fish, poultry or game, the holes to receive them being previously made with the point of a skewer. When small scallops of truffles, smoked tongue, ham, etc., are inlaid as garnish or ornament by incision, in fillets of any kind, they are said to be *contisés*. (*See also* CLOUTÉ.)

Contre-filet, F. A piece of boned sirloin.

Copeaux, F. Shavings. As *pommes en copeaux*—potato shavings.

Coq, F. Cock. *Coq de bruyère, F.* Woodcock. A bird allied to the snipe. *Coq-de-bruyère* is usually accepted as the French equivalent for grouse, and, as it is an exact rendering of heath-cock—a name once applied to red game in the north of England, it is good enough to pass muster. *Coq noir, F.*— Black game.

Coquille, F. Scallop, shell. *Coquilles (en)*—made-up dishes cooked and served in shells.

Corbeille, F. Basket.

Cordon Bleu. An ancient culinary distinction to very skilful female cooks who passed an exam. under the French Government, 1578–1830. It consisted of a medal suspended on a dark blue ribbon. The history of its adoption is traced to the time of Henry II., Charles II. and Louis XV. of France. It also describes a method of preparing veal escalopes with gruyère cheese and ham.

Core. To core an apple or pear is to remove the heart, which can be done when whole with a corer, and when cut in quarters with a knife.

Coriander. Coriandre, F. A sweet, aromatic seed, originally from the East. The powdered seeds from one of the ingredients of curry-powder.

Corlieu. (*See* COURLIS, F.) Curlew.

Corme, F. Shad apple, from which a kind of cider is made in France. Service berry, E. The word service is derived from *cerevisia,* a fermented drink.

Corn Salad. (*See* BOURCETTE, F.)

Corne d'Abondance, F. Cornucopia. Horn of Plenty.

Corned. Applied to salt boiled beef and pork. Derived from the word acorned (acorn-fed).

Corner le Diner, F. To blow the horn or sound the bell for dinner.

Cornet, F. Kind of thin wafer, usually made of flour, egg, cream, sugar, and honey.

Cornflour. A farina-made maize, or Indian corn, first invented by Messrs. Brown & Polson, in 1856, who define it as a refined starch specially prepared for food from Indian corn or maize.

Cornichon, F. (*See* GHERKIN.)

Cornish Pasty. A Cornish pasty is a baked, torpedo-shaped pasty, containing pork, mutton, rabbit, beef, and kidney, potatoes, onions, bacon, parsley, etc. Well cooked with light pastry, and when filled with finely-cut beef or mutton, it makes a palatable and satisying lunch or supper dish.

Corn-on-the-cob. Maïs frais au Naturel, F. Fresh corn cobs cooked in boiling salted water, approx. 15 mins., with fresh butter served separately.

Côte, F. A rib slice of beef or veal. The word côtelette is derived from *côte,* meaning a piece of meat with the portion of the rib attached. *Côtes de bœuf*—ribs of beef.

Côtelettes, F. Cutlets. Small pieces of meat cut from the neck of veal, mutton, lamb, or pork. Name also given to thin slices of lean meat cut from other parts.

Cottage Cheese. A creamy acid curd cheese which has a distinctive delicate flavour. It is made from pasteurized fat-free milk inoculated with a special curd to develop texture and flavour. Particularly valuable as a source of protein and riboflavin and easily digested.

Cougloff, F. Gugelhopf, G. A German cake; a kind of rich dough or yeast cake, with currants and raisins.

Coulibiac. Name of a Russian dish; a kind of fish-cake mixture wrapped up in brioche paste, and baked.

Coulis, F. A favourite liquid seasoning used for brown and white stews, and braise. Also the name of filtered soups, purées and certain creams. Formerly the name *coulis* referred to smooth sauces in general.

Coupe, F. Cup, drinking vessel, goblet. *Coupe St. Jacques*— A fruit salad served in glass cups with vanilla ice cream on top.

Coupé, F. Cut, broken, loose.

Coupe à Légumes, F.   Vegetable cutter.

Coupe à Pâte, F.   Pastry cutter.

Courge, Courgeon, F.   Squash. (*See* VEGETABLE MARROW.)

Courgette, F.   (*also Coucouzelle*). These are baby marrows picked from a variety of gourd before they are fully grown. They are called *zucchini* in the U.S.A.

Courlis, Corlis or **Corlieu,** F.   Curlew.

Couronne, F.   Crown. *En Couronne,* to dish up in the form of a crown.

Court-bouillon, F.   Stock, generally composed of white wine, water, pepper, salt, parsley, onions, etc., in which fish, etc., is cooked: *e.g., un court-bouillon de saumon, de carpe, etc.*

Cow-heel.   A great many invalid dishes are prepared from the feet of the ox or cow, as they are extremely nutritious.

Crab. Crabe, F.   An edible and tasty crustacean.

Crackers are very hard biscuits; when soaked used for pies, or when crumbled for making into pudding. In the United States of America the term crackers is used for biscuits generally.

Cracknels.   Biscuits made of paste which is boiled before it is baked. The biscuits, when boiled, curl up. After boiling, they are put into cold water to harden, dried, and finally baked.

Cranberry.   Airelle rouge, Airelle de marais, or canneberge, F.   This fruit grows in a cold climate, and on peaty bogs. In Siberia it is used in the manufacture of wine. Cranberries are chiefly imported from Russia and North America, although large quantities may be collected in a few parts of Britain and of Germany.

Crapaudine, F.   Word derived from crapaud toad, birds trussed and spread in the shape of a toad. A grating gridiron; hence *mettre à la crapaudine*—to grill, *e.g.,* pigeons or fowls, usually done "split" in spatchcock fashion. (*See* SPREAD EAGLE.)

Crawfish. Langouste, F.   A salt-water crustacean somewhat like the lobster, but much larger.

Crayfish. Ecrevisse, F.   Crayfish live entirely in fresh water, and are like a miniature lobster. They were much esteemed by the ancient Greeks and Romans, and are considered a great delicacy.

Crécy (Potage à la), F.   Crécy or carrot soup. A vegetable purée, said to have been invented by Baron Brisse. Dishes

48

named "à la Crécy" generally contain carrots in the form of a purée.

Crème, F. Cream. The fatty or oily part of milk. Used in butter and cheese making, as well as in the preparation of numerous sauces, soups, custards, puddings, pastry, and other food delicacies. Certain dishes are styled *à la crème,* meaning that a quantity of cream has been incorporated into the mixture before or after it is cooked. Meringues *à la crème* are meringue shells filled with whipped cream. The distinction between single and double cream is that double cream contains nearly three times as much butterfat as single cream and can be whipped easily; single cream is usually homogenized and will not whip unless a stiffly-whisked egg white is added.

Crèmeux, F. Creamy.

Crème bavaroise, F. Bavarian cream. (*See* BAVAROIS.)

Crème d'Orge, F. Finely ground barley. A white soup made of fine barley; a preparation sold in packets.

Crème de Riz, F. Finely ground rice. A white soup made of powdered rice; a preparation sold in packets.

Créole, F. A name given to certain dishes of which rice forms a part, as *Ananas à la créole.* Also to sweets masked with chocolate.

Crêpes, F. French pancakes.

Crépine, F. (*See* CAUL.)

Crépinette, F. A flat, oblong or sausage shape. Small portions of game or chicken mixture encased in pig's caul.

Cresson, F. Cress. A salad plant. There are several culinary plants belonging to this family. (*See* NASTURTIUM.)

Cresson de Fontaine, F. (*See* WATERCRESS.)

Crêtes, F. Giblets of poultry or game.

Crêtes de Coq, F. (*See* COCKS' COMBS, E.)

Crever, F. To burst or crack (generally used for rice).

Crevette, F. Shrimp.

Crevettes roses, F. Prawns.

Crimped. Recrépi, F. Large fish such as salmon and cod are sometimes crimped or slashed across at certain distances apart, to increase the firmness of the flesh.

Croissant, F. Crescent. Fancy bread in crescent or horse-shoe form.

Cromesquis. Kromeskis. Croquette shapes of chicken, game, lobster-meat, etc., rolled in thin slices of bacon, dipped in batter and fried.

Croquant, F. Crisp; crackling.

Croquantes, F. A transparent mixture of various kinds of fruit and boiled sugar.

Croque-en-bouche, F., is the name given to large set pieces for suppers or dinners, such as nougat, iced cakes, fruits, which are covered with boiled sugar so as to give them a brilliant appearance. The word means "crunch in the mouth."

Croquettes, F. Cork-shaped forms of minces of fowl, game, meat or fish, prepared with sauce to bind, shaped to fancy; generally egged, crumbed, and fried crisp.

Croquignolle, F. A kind of fondant (*petit four*) of the same composition as *croque-en-bouche*.

Crosnes de Japon, F. Chinese artichokes or stachys; the tubers of a plant originating in China or Japan.

Croustades, F. Shapes of bread fried, or baked paste crusts, used for serving delicate fish, game, ragoûts, minces, or meat entrées upon.

Croûte, F. Crust. A thick piece of fried bread upon which entrées, etc., are served.

Croûte-au-pot, F. Beef broth. A favourite soup of France, which has been famed for several centuries.

Croûtons, F. Thin slices of bread cut into shapes and fried or toasted, used for garnishing dishes.

Cru, F. Raw or uncooked.

Crumpet. Name of a tea-cake. In the North they are called "pikelets."

Cubat, Pierre. Name of a celebrated chef to the Emperor Alexander II. of Russia. His cooking was such a triumph that he received so much a head to prepare the Emperor's meals, no matter how large the number.

Cucumber. Concombre, F. A vegetable used in this country for salads, garnishing, and pickles, but in the East it is largely consumed as a staple article of food. (*See* GHERKIN.)

Cuillère de Cuisine, F. Wooden spoon. The use of wooden spoons is strongly recommended, especially for stirring sauces. The latter often contain certain acids which produce a dark colour, or an unpleasant taste if a metal spoon is used.

Cuisine, F. Kitchen. Cookery. *Faire la cuisine*—to cook or to dress victuals.

Cuisinier, F. A cook who prepares, cooks, and dresses food.

Cuisse, F. Leg, E. *Cuisse de volaille*—leg of chicken or fowl.

Cuisson, F. A method of slowly cooking meat. It is finished off by cooking in its own juice generally whilst in an oven.

Cuissot, F. The haunch. *Cuissot de veau, cuissot de cochon, cuissot de bœuf,* etc.

Cuit, F. Cooked.

Culinaire, F. This is applied to anything in connection with the kitchen or the art of cooking. A good cook is called *un artiste culinaire.*

Cullis, F. (*See* COULIS.)

Culotte, F. Rump, aitchbone of beef.

Cumberland. An English nobleman to whom was dedicated "Cumberland Sauce," prepared with currant jelly, orange-juice, English mustard, etc. Served principally with game.

Cumin, F. (*See* CARAWAY SEED.)

Curacao, F. A liqueur made of the zest of the rind of the bitter orange, cultivated in the island of Curacao in the Dutch West Indies and originally made there. Used for flavouring creams, jellies, ices, etc.

Curcuma, F. (*See* TURMERIC.)

Curd. That part of the milk which has been coagulated, usually by the aid of rennet, for the purpose of making cheese.

Cure. Saler, F. Saurer, F. Curing in culinary language means the drying or smoking of previously salted meat or fish.

Currants (dried). The name is derived from the fact they they were first imported from Corinth. The small seedless grapes from which they are made are originally red or blue. They form the principal article of export from Greece, where a very sweet kind of wine is also made from them.

Curry. Kari, F. An Indian condiment; a stew of meat, fish, or fowl; a sharp spiced sauce. Curry, as a dish, is of immemorial use in India. Its constituents vary much, according to the part of India. They are not always made with hot spices; some are quite mild. The word Curry is derived from the Tamil *Kari,* the leaf of a plant belonging to the orange tribe, or from the Hindu *Khura,* palatable.

Cussy, Baron de. A French nobleman and a great gourmet, who occupied an important post under Napoleon I. Born 1765, died 1837. Several dishes are named "à la Cussy."

51

Custard. A composition of milk and eggs, usually sweetened and flavoured, parboiled, or baked.

Custard Apple. Pomme cannelle, F. It is a native of the West Indies. The inner pulp is yellow and of the consistence of custard. In outward appearance it is netted all over, and is dark-brown or greenish in colour.

Custard Marrow. A vareity of marrow which has a most delicate flavour; it is round in shape, resembling a large flat apple. When cooked, it resembles a custard in consistency, hence its name.

Cutlets. Côtelettes, F. Neck chops (best end) of mutton, lamb, pork, or veal. Cutlets are also made of chicken, lobster, salmon, and pheasant.

Cygne, F. Swan.

Cymling. Summer squash or marrow.

Dab. Limande, F. A small flat fish of a dark brown colour allied to the flounder. Mostly served like fried sole, and even substituted therefore by unscrupulous restaurateurs.

Dabchick. A small water-fowl.

Dace. A small river fish of a silvery colour.

Dainty. Friand or délicieux, F. Pleasing to the palate, artistically arranged, daintily dressed articles of food.

Dampfundeln, G. A typical German dish. It consists of dumplings of bread dough, enriched with butter, sugar, and eggs, which, after being par-cooked in milk, are steamed in the oven, and served with custard sauce, stewed fruit, etc.

Damson. (Sometimes called damascene, after the name of the town of Damascus.) A small black plum, considered the best for cooking.

Damson Cheese. A preserve made by boiling damsons to a pulp, and then boiling again with an equal quantity of sugar. When cold it is of the consistence of cheese.

Dandelion. Dent de lion or Pissenlit, F. Lion's tooth. A well-known wild herb, which is also cultivated for salads. The young leaves are used raw, but may also be cooked like spinach.

Danish Blue Cheese. A cheese of the Gorgonzola-Roquefort variety but less pungent.

Dariole, F. A kind of small entrée pâté, composed of a compound of forcemeat or mince, baked or steamed in small moulds. Certain small tarts are also so called. The name usually applies to the shape of the moulds. Also some kinds of cheese cakes are called darioles. Kettner assets that a dariole means something made of milk. Origin of the word unknown.

Darne, F. A slice. The middle cut of large fish, salmon or cod.

Dartois, F. A kind of French pastry (puff-paste and jam), known also as *gâteau à la manon*.

Dates. Dattes, F. The fruit of the date-tree (date-palm). The best dates come from Tunis. In Africa they form a staple food. The so-called date wine, prepared in Africa, is made of dates and water, and has a certain analogy with Maderia.

Daube, F. *En daube* or *à la daube*—name applied to meats or poultry braised.

Daubière, F. An oval-shaped stewpan in which meats or birds are to be daubed, stewed or braised.

Dauphin, F. The name of a potato dish similar to *Pommes Anna* except that the potatoes are cut in julienne strips.

Dauphine, F. A style of garnish; also name of a kind of dough-nut, beignets, etc. Known in Germany as *Berliner Pfannkuchen*.

Daurade, F. A sea-fish about 18 inches long resembling the bream. It is sometimes called sea bream (*brême de mer*). Its flesh is white and of good flavour. Mostly baked, or cooked in white caper or tomato sauce, but may also be fried. Not to be confounded with *Dorade* (*q.v.*)

Decant (to). To pour a liquor which has a sediment from its original receptacle into another without transferring the lees. *Decanter*—a glass-stoppered bottle into which wine is decanted.

Deer. Cerf, F. One of the undomesticated animals which still form part of our diet. There are several kinds of deer—

53

red deer and fallow deer are the best known in the United Kingdom but many others are used elsewhere.

Déglacer, F.   A term which means to dilute the concentrated juices in a pan, in which various foodstuffs have been roasted, braised or shallow fried.

Dégraisser, F.   To take off the grease from soups, etc.

Déjeuner, F.   Breakfast. The first meal of the day.

Déjeuner à la Fourchette, F.   A meat breakfast or luncheon.

Déjeuner de Noce, F.   Wedding breakfast.

Demi-deuil (en), F.   A culinary expression. When white meats such as veal, sweetbreads or fowl are larded with truffles, they are called *en demi-deuil.* The meaning is "half-mourning."

Demidoff, F.   Name of a Russian nobleman. Several dishes are distinguished by this name.

Demi-glace, F.   Name of a brown sauce of rather thinner consistency than an ordinary sauce, a refined *Espagnole* sauce, usually finished with Sherry; also of a cream ice very popular in Paris.

Demi-tasse, F.   Half cup. A current expression for a small cup of black coffee or bouillon.

Dent-de-lion, F.   (*See* DANDELION).

Dépecer, F.   Découper. To carve; to cut in pieces.

D'Eslignac, F.   A French nobleman after whom a clear soup is named.

Dés, F.   Dice. *En dés*—cut into dice shapes.

Désosser, F.   To bone; to remove the bones from meat, poultry or game.

Dessécher, F.   To stir a purée, pulp or paste with a wooden spoon whilst it is on the fire, until it becomes loosened from the pan.

Dessert, F.   The remains of a meal. Now indicating fruits and sweetmeats served after dinner. The ancient Greeks and Romans already knew this course as being the custom of prolonging banquets.

Devilled. Diablé, F.   Generally applied to broiled or grilled fish or meat, with the addition of very hot condiments, and sometimes a highly-seasoned spiced sauce.

Dewberry. The creeping blackberry. A species of the French *mûre des haies.*

Dholl or **Dhal.**   A kind of pulse much used in India for kedgeree, or as a kind of porridge. In England it is best represented by split peas or lentils.

Diablé, F., from Diable (Devil). (*See* DEVILLED.)

Diavolini. Italian name for small devilled rice or farina cakes, fried.

Dibs. Arab name for wine juice reduced to a very thick and luscious syrup.

Diète, F. Diet. Any specially prescribed food or meals.

Digby Chicks. A kind of pilchard or small herring, called by the fishermen who catch them "Nova Scotia sprats." They are named after Digby, a seaport in Nova Scotia.

Dill. A hardy biennial plant, possessing powerful flavouring properties, used in salads and soups.

Dinde, Dindon, F. (*See* TURKEY.) Hen and cock respectively. *Dindonneau*—young turkey. Cock turkey.

Dinde farcie. Stuffed turkey.

Dinde piquée. Larded turkey.

Dinde rôtie. Roast turkey.

Diner, F. Dinner. *L'heure du dîner,* dinner hour, in Henry VIII.'s time was at 11 a.m. The principal meal of the day, which usually comprises a judicious selection of food in season. The word dinner is supposed to be a corruption of *dix-heures,* indicating the time at which the old Normans partook of their principal meal, which was 10 a.m. Since then the hour has got gradually later.

Diner mi-Carème, F. Lenten Dinner.

Dinner. Diner, F. (*See* DINER.)

Doie de Veau, F. Calf's liver.

Dolmas. A Turkish dish of chopped meat, etc., wrapped in fig leaves and stewed.

Dorade, F. A fish found in the tropical seas, and seen in our aquariums, gold fish and red fish (*carassus doré*). Not to be confounded with *Daurade* (*q.v.*)

Doré, F. Brushed over with beaten egg yolks. (*Dorure.*) Bien dorée—well coloured.

Dormant or **Surtout de Table,** F. Decorative objects which are left on the table to the end of a meal.

Dorure, F. Yolks of eggs beaten, used for brushing over pastry, etc.

Double Cream, Crème double, F. Cream with not less than 48% butterfat content. (*See also* CREAM.)

Douce-amère, F. Bittersweet. *Doux-ce*—sweet.

Doucette, F. Corn salad.

Douilles mobiles, F.   Movable tubes, adjusted on forcing, or savoy bag, used for the purpose of filling and decorating.

Doux, douce, F.   Sweet.

Dragées, F.   Sugar plum. A kind of sweetmeat made of fruits, small pieces of rinds or aromatic roots, covered with a coating of icing. Also small lentiform pieces of plain chocolate.

Drawn Butter. Beurre fondu, F.   Melted butter, sometimes served in place of sauce.

Dress (to).   To pare, clean, trim, etc.; to dish up into good shape. Dressed vegetables indicate vegetables cooked in rich style and dished neatly.

Dressé or **Garni.**   Dressed or garnished.

Dripping.   The fat of meat which exudes while it is being roasted or baked.

Du Barry.   Name given to a rich cauliflower soup; oysters served in potato cases, and other dishes are also named after Madame du Barry.

Dublin Bay Prawns, Langoustine, F.   Scampi, IT.   These are large prawns which are prepared in the same way as shrimps; all recipes for freshwater crayfish and most other shellfish may be used especially for the largest of them. These are often known as Jumbo Scampi and are sepecially popular when deep-fried—*scampi frite.*

Dubois, Urbain.   Name of a clever chef de cuisine, inventor of numerous dishes, author of "La Cuisine Classique," etc.; for many years chef to the German Emperor William I. Born 1818, died 1901.

Duchesse, F.   Duchess. A name given to a mashed potato preparation, variously shaped and baked in the oven.

Duck. Canard, F.   There is a great variety of these birds. Of the domestic ducks, the Aylesbury commands the highest price. The Rouen duck is larger, but its flesh is considered inferior in flavour.

Duglère, F.   A famous French chef who invented the method of serving soles or turbot which is poached with *tomatos concassées,* chopped onions, white wine, fish stock and chopped parsley. The cooking liquor is reduced and finished with butter to make the sauce. Also responsible for creating *pommes anna.*

Dumas. Alexandre.   Name of a famous French author, editor of the "Dictionnaire de Cuisine." Born 1803, died 1870.

Dumplings. Quenelles, F.   Knödel, G.   Ball shapes of bread dough (Norfolk dumpling), suet paste, or short crust enclosing apples. Also applied to farce or forcemeat shapes; *i.e.,* quenelles.

Dunelm. A dish of braised mutton or veal, originating in Durham, of which Dunelm is the abbreviated Latin name.

Duxelles or D'Uxelles, F. Name of a French marquis, a great gourmand and gastronomer, who lived at the end of the 17th century. Author of an excellent book on French cookery. A savoury purée or mince and a sauce are known under this name.

Eau, F. Water. *Eau de fleur d'oranger*—orange-flower water. *Eau de vie*—spirits of wine, old brandy, etc.

Eau de Vie de Prunelle, F. Sloe gin.

Ebarber, F. To remove the exterior parts of a piece of meat or fish.

Ebullition, F. A liquid which is on the boiling point. *Chauffer à l'ébullition* means heated until boiling.

Echalote, F. Shallot, E. Is a kind of mild onion used for seasoning soups and made dishes; also used for flavouring sauces and salads.

Echauder, F. To steep in boiling water. This is often done with fowls or game, as it will facilitate the removing of the feathers or hair.

Éclair, F. A French pastry filled with cream.

Éclanche, F. Shoulder of mutton.

Écossaise (à l'), F. Scottish style.

Écrevisse, F. (*See* CRAYFISH.)

Écumé. Skimmed. *Ecumoire*—skimming ladle or perforated spoon.

Edible Birds' Nests. (*See* BIRDS' NESTS.)

Edible Frog. Grenouille, F. These frogs are eaten in France and the south of Germany. The hind legs are considered

57

a great delicacy, and in flavour resemble the flesh of a young rabbit.

Edible Snail. (*See* ESCARGOT, F.)

Eel. Anguille, F. A nutritious fish whose flesh has a particularly rich flavour. There are several kinds of eel, both fresh and salt water, but the silver eel is considered the best. When in want of food the common eel will leave its native elements and wander about the fields by night in search of snails or other prey, and will often betake itself to isolated ponds for the sake of a change of residence. Smoked eel has a pleasant flavour and is often served as an appetizer.

Eel-pout. (*See* LOTTE.)

Egg. Oeuf, F. An important article of food. Those from the domestic fowl are the most popular; other eggs used for cooking are ducks' eggs, plovers' eggs, and penguin eggs, the last two being considered real delicacies.

Egg Nog. Name of an invalid drink, also of an American drink.

Egg-plant. (*See* AURBERGINE, F.)

Egg-plum. Also known as "Magnum bonum." There are two kinds, one red, the other white and yellow. Each variety is divided into several kinds bearing different names. The flesh of the fruit is firm, not very juicy, but of a splendid flavour.

Egyptienne, F. Usually denotes that lentils are featured.

Eland. A large antelope.

Elderberry. Sureau, F. The small black berry of the elder-tree found all over Europe, Northern Africa, and Asia. It is used for making a wholesome wine which, drunk hot at night, is considered a preventative of and cure for colds.

Elmassia. A Turkish dish, made from calves' feet.

Émincé, F. Finely sliced or shredded.

Emonder, F. Blanch, *e.g.*, to steep almonds in boiling water in order to peel them.

Emulsion. A liquid containing minute drops of oil or fat in more or less stable suspension. This is brought by emulsification (the breaking down of fats with liquids). The ingredients concerned are usually raised to a uniform temperature and subjected to violent agitation. The name also applies in cookery to Mayonnaise and Hollandaise sauce.

En, F. In, denoting "served in," as *cailles en caisses*—quails in cases; *en casserole*—in a pipkin, etc.

Enchilada. A South American pancake of maize flour,

(tortilla) fried in hot fat, and then filled or spread with a spicy hot sauce based mainly on tomatoes and chilli powder. Popular in Mexico.

En Croûte, F.   Encrusted, wrapped or enclosed in paste prior to cooking.

En Papillote, F.   Fish, meat or birds wrapped in greased paper, in which they are cooked and sent to table.

Endive, F.   (*See* CHICORY.)

English Bamboo.   The name given to a pickle, made from the young shoots of the elder-tree, salted and dried, with a pickle vinegar poured over them.

En Tasse, F.   Served in cups. Chiefly applied to clear soups.

Entrecôte, F.   Name of a sirloin steak cut from the middle part of the loin or sometimes the rib of beef. *Entrecôte double*—a double entrecôte steak; *Entrecôte minute* — an *Entrecôte* which has been batted out thinly.

Entrée, F.   A course of dishes, or corner dish for the first course; the conventional term for hot or cold side-dishes. Also defined as dishes generally served with a sauce.

Entremets, F.   Dainty dishes of vegetables or hot and cold sweets and after-dinner savouries served as second course.

Enzyme.   A complex organic substance produced by animals and plants. In solution enzymes produce fermentation and chemical changes in other substances, apparently without undergoing any change itself. Their effect is retarded by low temperature and destroyed by higher than body temperature.

Epanada.   Spanish and Portuguese term for panada (*q.v.*).

Épaule, F.   Shoulder. *Épaule de mouton*—shoulder of mutton.

Eperlan, F.   Smelt. A highly-esteemed sea-fish.

Eperlans frits, F.   Fried smelts.

Épice, F.   Spice, seasoning. Aromatic plants or their seeds.

Epicure.   One addicted to the luxury of eating and drinking.

Epigrammes, F.   Verbally, a concise and pointed poem or saying. Used as a culinary term for small fillets of poultry and game, and breast of lamb or mutton, prepared as entrées. Also defined as a dish of alternate cutlets of the neck and breast.

Épinard, F.   (*See* SPINACH.)

Érable, F.   Maple-tree. *Sirop d'érable*—maple syrup. *Sucre d'érable*—maple sugar.

Escabescia.   A Spanish dish of partridges highly seasoned.

Escallop.   (*See* SCALLOP.)

59

Escalope, F.   Collop. Thin round steaks of veal, usually egged, crumbed, and fried. Obsolete *cascalope,* meaning thin slices of any kind of meat.

Escargot, F.   Edible Snail. Considered as a delicacy in China and France. The continental edible snail differs both in colour and size from the usual garden snail of this country, where it is not greatly esteemed as a food. The edible snail was brought from southern Europe to this country in the 17th century, and is still found in districts where chalk abounds. Luxurious Romans thought most highly of such snails, and even fattened them on a certain kind of meal and boiled wine.

Escarole, F.   Broad-leaved endive. Chicory.

Escoffier, A.   A celebrated French maître chef, author of "Le Guide Culinaire" and "A Guide to Modern Cookery."

Espagnole, F.   Spanish. A rich brown sauce; the foundation of nearly all brown sauces; classified as the main brown grand sauce, or *sauce mère.*

Essence.   The virtue extracted from any food substance.

Estouffade, F.   Expression for a way of cooking meats slowly with very little liquid, in a covered stewpan. Braised, stewed or steamed. Also the name of a good quality light brown stock.

Estragon, F.   (*See* TARRAGON.)

Esturgeon, F.   Sturgeon. A very large fish, usually salted and smoked.

Étamine, F.   Tammy cloth.

Étouffé, Etuvé, F.   (*See* ESTOUFFADE.)

Extra-fin, F.   Of the best quality. Denoting the quality of articles; also *surfin, trés fin, fin,* etc.

Fagot, F. (*See* BOUQUET GARNI.)

Faggots. A savoury preparation of pig's liver, fat pork, onions, breadcrumbs, herbs, etc., covered with caul, and slowly baked in a tin. The mixture is divided into squares usually before cooking.

Faire Revenir, F. A term often used in French cookery books; its meaning is to partly fry, meat or vegetables being tossed, *i.e.,* slightly browned without actually cooking them.

Faire Suer, F. To cook meat in a covered stewpan with no liquor except the juices which ooze from the meat.

Faisan, F. Pheasant (*which see*).

Faisan piqué. Larded pheasant.

Fanchonnettes, F. Small custard tartlets covered with meringue froth.

Farce. F. Forcemeat or stuffing, from the Latin word *farcire,* to fill, to stuff. From this is derived the word *farcimen,* the sausage. A *farce* need not necessarily contain meat, though the English translation makes the presence of meat essential. *Farci*—stuffed.

Farine, F. (*See* FLOUR.) *Farineé,* F. Powdered or dredged with flour.

Fascine, F. Bundle, *e.g.,* a bundle of asparagus.

Faséole, Féverole, F. Kidney-bean.

Fat. Graisse, F. The oily or fatty part of animal bodies.

Faubonne, F. A vegetable purée soup seasoned with savoury herbs.

Faux, Fausse, F. Mock, false, as *fausse tortue,* mock, turtle.

Fayol or **Fayot,** F. A French kidney-bean, dried.

Fécule, F. A very fine flour used for binding soups and sauces. *Fécule de pommes de terre*—potato flour. *Fécule de riz*—rice flour.

Fendre, F. To split, as *fendre un poulet pour griller,* to split a chicken for broiling.

Fennel. Fenouil, F. An aromatic plant, generally used in fish sauces, blanched, and chopped. There are several species of this plant. That found in India (*Fœniculum vulgare*) is cultivated for its sweet, warm, and aromatic flavour.

Fenouillette, F.   A little russet apple with a flavour of fennel.

Fenugreek. Fenugrec, F.   The ground seeds of this plant form one of the ingredients in curry-powder. Fenugreek is largely cultivated in India as a fodder-plant, and it derives its name from *Fœnum Grœcum,* Greek hay, of which the English name is a corruption.

Fermentation.   A chemical change included in a solution by a ferment such as yeast. Many low forms of life, such as bacteria, can induce fermentative changes in various liquids. Beer, wine, alcohol and vinegar are classed as fermented products.

Fermière (à la), F.   Farmhouse Style. As a garnish young carrots, turnips, onions and celery are usually included, often cut in "paysanne."

Feuillé, F.   With leaf garnishing.

Feuillage, F.   Leaves.

Feuilletage, F.   Puff-paste.

Fèves, F.   Beans. *Fèves de marais*—broad beans.

Fèves d'Espagne.   Scarlet runners, string beans.

Fidelini.   A kind of straight vermicelli paste.

Fieldfare. Grive, F.   A migratory bird of the thrush tribe. Found in England in winter.

Fig. Figue, F.   The fruit of the *ficus carica.*   In the unripe state, figs contain a bitter juice, which is replaced with saccharine matter when they are ripe. In favourable seasons some fig trees near Worthing, said to have been planted by order of Thomas à Becket, yield enormous quantities of fruit. The Smyrna figs are considered the finest. Used fresh for compotes, and dried as dessert or in puddings.

Figaro, F.   Name of a cold sauce, a mixture of mayonnaise and tomato.

Filbert. Aveline, F.   A fine dessert nut of the hazel kind. Largely cultivated in Kent.

Filé, F.   Spun, stringed, as *sucre filé.*

Filet, F.   Fillet. The under-cut of a loin of beef, mutton, veal, pork, and game. Also boned breasts of poultry birds, and the boned sides of fish are called fillets. *Filet Mignon*—small daintily cut fillet of beef, or the fillet from the underneath of a loin of lamb. *Filet en Chevreuil*—fillet of venison or roebuck. *Filet en Chevreuil*—mutton cooked and served in imitation of venison. *Filet de bœuf*—fillet of beef. *Filet de veau*—fillet of veal.

Filtering. This is straining liquids by causing them to pass through various filtering materials.

Financière, F. A ragoût of truffles, cocks' combs, cock's kernel, etc., used as garnish for entrées.

Fines-herbes, F. Fine herbs. A combination of finely-chopped fresh herbs, parsley, chervil and tarragon. Mostly used in omelets, salads, and sauces.

Firmity. (*See* FRUMENTY.)

Fish. Poisson, F. Fish stew is called matelote.

Flageolet, F. A green haricot bean.

Flamande (à la), F. Flemish Style.

Flamber, F. To singe poultry or game; also used to describe the operation involved in preparing certain dishes, *i.e.*: to set alight with brandy etc. *Flamber au Cognac.*

Flan, F. A French custard tart; open fruit tarts.

Flanc, Flanchet, F. Flank (or beef or codfish).

Flank of Veal. The flank lies between the breast and the leg. It is generally used for stewing.

Flapjack. Tôt-fait, F. A kind of hasty pancake.

Flavouring. Seasoning. Certain ingredients consisting principally of spices, herbs, and essences, used in cookery to impart taste or flavour to food in order to render it more palatable.

Flétan, Grand Flétan, F. Halibut, and similar fish.

Fleurons, F. Little half-moon shapes of baked puff paste used for garnishing.

Flip. A drink consisting of eggs beaten up with sugar, beer or wine, and some spirit. A favourite drink in cold weather.

Flitch. Un quartier de lard, F. A side or pork, salted and cured.

Flounder. Carrelet, F. A small flat sea-fish of delicate flavour, found in the North Sea.

Flour. Farine, F. Flour consists of crushed or decorticated grain reduced to powder. Wheaten flour is made from wheat, cornflour from maize or Indian corn, rice flour from rice. Barley, oats, and maize yield flour deficient in gluten, which, therefore, cannot be made into upright loaves.

Flummery. Name given to a cold sweet dish, made mainly of cereals, originally of oatmeal set in a mould and turned out. Dutch flummery is made with gelatine or isinglass, egg

63

yolks, and flavourings; Spanish flummery is made of cream, rice flour, cinnamon and sugar.

Flute, F.   A flute or finger-shaped roll.

Fogasch or **Fogàs.**   Name of a fish of delicate flavour, found in Hungarian lakes. Usually served with paprika or hollandaise sauce.

Foie de Veau, F.   Calf's liver.

Foie-Gras, F.   Fat goose liver.

Foncé, F.   Dark coloured. Lined, bottomed (as a mould with paste lining).

Fond, F.   Strong gravy, meat stock, bottom, as in *fond d'artichaut.*

Fondant, F.   Melting. A kind of icing; French dessert bonbons.

Fondu, F.   Melted.

Fondue, F.   A preparation of melted cheese, originally made in Switzerland. A cheese savoury.

Fontaine, F.   Fountain. Spring. *Faire une fontaine*—(to make a well or hollow in the flour in the bowl or on the table.)

Forbidden Fruit. (*See* SHADDOCK.)   Small shaddocks received this name from a conjecture that it may have been the fruit which Eve took in the Garden of Eden.

Forcemeat. Farce, F., *i.e.,* pounded or finely minced meat, etc., for stuffing meat or birds. The word is also applied to veal stuffing, which usually consists of suet, parsley, etc. Sage and onion, oyster, chestnut and truffle stuffings are also included under this name.

Fore Quarter of Lamb. Quartier d'Agneau, F.   The fore quarter of young lamb is generally considered the best joint and consists of the shoulder, breast and neck.

Forestière, F.   Usually means that mushrooms are included in some form.

Fouetté, F.   Whipped with the whisk.

Four, F.   Oven. *Four (au).* Baked.

Fourchette, F.   Fork, E.   First manufactured in England in 1608; its use was ridiculed at the time.

Fourré, F.   Coated with sugar, cream, etc.; also applied to filled or stuffed birds, etc.

Fowl. Volaille, F.

Fraise, F.   Strawberry. Also the mesentery of a calf or lamb; the fleshy excrescence (wattle) under the throat of a turkey.

64

Fraiser la Pâte, F.   To plait; to make rough; to ruffle.

Fraisure.   (*See* FRESSURE, F.)

Framboise, F.   (*See* RASPBERRY.)

Française (à la), F.   This is, generally speaking, applied to a number of dishes of French origin. The term is used for dishes cooked in a simple manner as to those of the most elaborate finish. With the exception of a few grills and soups, the term cannot be taken as signifying anything in particular, because the preparation as well as the garnish varies in almost every case. (*See also* FRENCH SURNAMES TO DISHES.)

Francatelli.   Name of an eminent chef (1805–1876), author of the "Cook's Guide" and the "Modern Cook," pupil of A. Carème, chef at the Reform Club, and to her late Majesty Queen Victoria.

Francatu, F.   A russet apple.

Frangipane.   A substitute for custards made of eggs, milk, some flour, with an addition of lemon-rind, rum, brandy, and vanilla, etc., to flavour. An excellent confectioner's custard for filling tartlets, etc., is also made in this way and under this name. The French often use it for covering fruit tarts.

Frappé, F.   Iced (used when cooling champagne).

French Beans. Haricot verts, F.   (*See* BEANS.)

French Coffee.   Coffee with brandy, slightly whipped double cream and brown sugar. The sugar is dissolved in brandy in a glass, coffee is then added and the cream poured over the back of a spoon into the coffee so that it floats on top; this is often prepared in front of the customer.

French Fried.   A term used to describe chipped potatoes cooked in deep fat.

French Rolls.   This bread is superior in quality to ordinary household bread, as the dough should contain milk and sometimes butter. The rolls are baked and made up in various forms.

French Surnames to Dishes.—The French Cuisine has a considerable number of thoroughly descriptive and well-understood surnames given to dishes, all of which come under the title of *à la Française*; many of these are named after some peculiarities favoured in the provinces of France. Surnames derived from French towns, from certain countries, and from past and present patrons of the culinary art under whose influence many dishes have been invented, and in some cases actually prepared, are also very numerous, and, with few exceptions, most significant and expressive. There are many dishes which derive their names merely from sauces with which they are served or dressed, and have no reference to the mode of preparation. Thus dishes styled *à la Béchamel, à la Bordelaise, à la demi-glace, à l'Espagnole,* etc., are, as a rule, names merely derived from these sauces. The old school strictly adheres to all such names; they are universally adopted by all good chefs, and recognised by connoisseurs and gourmets alike. It must, however, be stated that many of these names are either abused or misused by some chefs, many of them having their own formula of preparation, which are presented under names that differ considerably from the original methods for which these names were intended as symbols of typical preparations. Dishes thus altered are therefore hard to recognise if served under a well-known name, but in a different style; they lose all the culinary charm or its significance, they puzzle and fog the diner who is acquainted with the gastronomic law in respect to the names and characteristics of dishes; and, to say the least, they also confuse cooks who may be called upon to prepare dishes produced and served under wrong titles.

Fressure, F.   Haslet or lights, *e.g., fressure d'âgneau*—lamb's lights.

Friand, F.   An epicure; a dainty person.

Friandines, F.   Small round patties containing mince.

Friandises, F.   Name given to small dessert dainties, petits fours, etc.

Friar's Omelet.   A baked omelet prepared with apples stewed to a pulp, eggs, and sugar.

Fricandeau, F.   Braised cushion or fillet of veal, larded. This dish is supposed to have been invented by Jean de Carême, who was the direct ancestor of the famous Carême. He was cook to Pope Leo X. This Pontiff possessed magnificent tastes; he fostered the genius of Raphael the painter, and encouraged also the genius which could discover a fricandeau.

Fricandelles, F.   Small thin braised steaks of veal or game.

Fricassée, F.   Fricasseed. A white stew of chicken, rabbit, or veal.

Frisé, F.   Curled. As *chou frisé*—curled Savoy cabbage.

Frit or **Frite,** F.   Fried. *Friteau* or *fritot*—anything dipped in frying batter, and fried in deep fat.

Frittata. An Italian dish; a kind of rolled pancake crumbed and fried in fat.

Fritter. Beignet, F. Anything dipped in batter, crumbed or egged, and fried.

Friture, F. This word has two significations; it applies to the fat, which may be oil lard or dripping in which articles are fried. Further, it is applied to anything that has been fried, such as egged and crumbed fried fish, fried potatoes, croquettes or rissoles, being pre-eminently popular under this term.

Frog. Grenouille, F. (*See* EDIBLE FROG.)

Froid, F. Cold. "Service froid," cold service, etc.

Fromage, F. Cheese, *Fromage de Cochon*—brawn. *Fromage glacé*—an ancient expression for an ice cream or frozen pudding in the form of a cheese.

Fromageon. A white cheese made of sheep's milk. (South of France product.).

Frosting. A culinary term; to make certain dishes appear like frost. It consists of whipped whites of egg spread roughly over the dish, dredged with castor sugar, and baked in a cool oven. Also icing for cakes (U.S.).

Frothing of roast joints, or roasts in general. Dredging the surface with flour and briskly heating it to a brown colour.

Fructose. Fruit sugar, *e.g.,* honey, etc.

Frumenty. Once a Lord Mayor's dish, and a staple food of our robust ancestors; it is wheat or barley boiled. Eaten with honey, sugar, milk or treacle.

Fry (to). Frire, F. A cooking process by immersing articles into very hot fat till done. To cook in hot fat, butter or oil.

Fumé, F. Smoked. Smoked hams, bacon, fish, etc.

Fumet, F. The flavour or essence of game, fish or any highly-flavoured concentrated substance used to impart a rich flavour to certain dishes or sauces.

Fumet de poisson, F. Fish stock.

Gaelic Coffee. As for French Coffee, (*q.v.*) substituting whisky for brandy.

Galantine, F. A dish of white meat, rolled, pressed, and glazed, served cold. A fowl or breast of veal, boned and stuffed with forcemeat—*i.e.,* farce, tongue, truffle, etc.

Galantine de dinde, F. Boned turkey or turkey galantine.

Galette, F. A kind of French pastry. A species of light, round, flat-shaped breakfast rolls. Also the name of a potato dish made from *Duchesse* mixture in the shape of medallions and shallow fried.

Galimafrée, F. A kind of ragoût made of cold meat. Origin of word unknown.

Game. Gibier, F. Under this name are included pheasants, partridges, grouse, blackcock, heath-fowl, moor-fowl, bustards, hares, etc. Snipe, quails and landrails, though not called game, are protected.

Ganneymede. A catering system for the service of food mainly employed in hospitals. Conveyor belts are used and metal pellets used to keep food hot after it has been plated. (Food may also be kept cold).

Garbure, F. A kind of maigre broth made with bread and vegetables. Originally a soup of cabbage and bacon.

Garçon, F. Waiter. *Premier garçon*—head-waiter. *Garçon de salle*—restaurant waiter.

Garde manger, F. Larder or meat safe. Also applied to the person in charge of the cold meat room or larder; larder cook.

Gardon, F. Roach.

Garfish. A fish which resembles mackeral, but is drier.

Gargotage, F. Badly dressed victuals. *Gargote*—common or cheap restaurant. *Gargotier*—keeper of a common cookshop; a bad cook.

Garlic. Ail, F. A root-plant with a pungent taste. Like onions, chives, and shallots, it possesses medicinal virtues, being cooling to the system, increasing saliva and gastric juices, stimulating, and digestive. First imported from Sicily.

Garlic, it is said, was cultivated from the earliest ages. It formed part of the rations of the Egyptian pyramid builders, and in this way, perhaps, the Jews acquired their fondness for it. The Roman soldiers were given garlic as an excitant. It is useful in cooking, sauce-making, etc.

Garnishing. Garnature, F. As a culinary term, it means to decorate a dish with edibles of ornamental appearance. *Garni*, F. Garnished, filled or stuffed.

Gasterea. Goddess of Gastronomy, presiding over everything appertaining to the preservation of life. From the Greek *gaster,* the stomach.

Gastronome, F. Epicure.

Gastronomie, F. Gastronomy. The art of good living. Strictly speaking, meaning the science of life, through which we discover what food, under various circumstances, is best suited; and it teaches us the effect it bears upon man individually or a nation.

Gâteau, F. A round, square or oval-shaped flat cake, generally decorated; essentially a rich cake made of well-beaten eggs, butter, sugar, dough, etc.

Gaufre, F. Wafer, waffle; a light biscuit; baked or fried in specially-constructed Gaufre moulds. These consist of two opposed plates, and are worked by handles. *Gaufrier*, F.—A waffle iron.

Gazpacho. A Spanish clear soup, flavoured with garlic, garnished with cucumber, tomatoes, sweet peppers and small round slices of bread, served very cold.

Gelant, F. Jellied or partly freezing.

Gélatine, F. A manufactured article, used for giving solidity to liquids. It swells when placed in water and becomes translucent, but does not dissolve to any great extent, although it passes into solution upon heating. It is prepared from the skin, hoofs, and other tissues of various quadrupeds. Used in the preparation of sweet and savoury jellies.

Gelée, F. Jelly. Gelatinized juice of fruit or meat.

Gelinotte, F. Hazel-hen.

Genièvre, F. Juniper-berry. A blue-black berry, possessing a peculiar aromatic flavour, used as a flavouring condiment in mirepoix, marinades, etc.; also used in syrups and liqueurs. The essential oil gives the well-known flavour to gin, Hollands, Schiedam, Schnapps, etc.

Génoise, F.   Genoese Style. Also the name of a kind of sponge cake; a rich brown fish sauce.

George IV.   An English monarch with a partiality for roast neck of mutton and bubble-and-squeak.

Gervais, F.   A sweet French cream cheese.

Ghee.   An Indian word for clarified butter.

Gherkin. Cornichon, or petit concombre, F.   Small cucumbers pickled with salt or vinegar. They are served as *hors d'œuvre,* and used for salads and sauces as well as for decorative purposes.

Gibelotte, F.   Rabbit stew.

Gibier, F.   Game; animals taken in the chase. (*See* GAME.)

Giblets. Abatis, F.   The trimmings of poultry (neck, pinions, liver, heart, etc.). Those from geese, turkeys, fowls, and ducks are principally used for pies, stews, and soups.

Gigot, F.   *Gigot de mouton*—leg of mutton. *Gigot d'âgneau*—leg of a lamb.

Gigot à l'Ail, F.   This is a favourite dish in France. The garlic is sometimes boiled in three separate waters before the cloves are inserted into the leg of mutton; this greatly modifies the strong taste and penetrating flavour and smell of garlic.

Gigot à Sept Heures or **Gigot à la Cuillère** is a leg of mutton which has been cooked for seven hours, when it may be carved with a spoon.

Gimblettes, F.   A kind of French pastry prepared in the shape of a ring, and similar to *croque-en-bouche*.

Gin.   A spirit flavoured by certain aromatic substances, generally sweetened, but also sold unsweetened.

Ginger. Gingembre, F.   Ginger is the root of a plant, a native of East and West Indies. This plant grows to the height of about three feet, and when its stalks are withered the roots are gathered, separated, scraped, washed, bleached, and dried ready for use or exportation. It is also ground or preserved whole for various culinary purposes. Ginger was known to the Romans, and is said by Pliny to have been brought from Arabia.

Gingerbread. Pain d'épice, F.   Gingerbread made of rye-flour, honey, ginger, and other spices, was sold in Paris as early as the 14th century. It was probably introduced into England in the reign of Henry the Fourth, and shortly afterwards treacle was used in making it, instead of honey. Gingerbread made with treacle being darker than that made with honey it was covered with gold-leaf or gilt paper to disguise its colour; hence arose our familiar proverb about taking "the gilt off the gingerbread."

Girofle, F. (*See* CLOVE.)

Gitana (à la). Gipsy fashion.

Glace, F. Ice. Also applied to concentrated stock—*i.e.*, meat glaze. *Glacé,* F.—Frozen, iced.

Glace de sucre (Glace royale). Icing sugar; very fine dust sugar; mixed with white of egg it is called Royal Icing.

Glace de viande, F. Meat extract or glaze. Stock or gravy reduced to the thickness of jelly; used for glazing cooked meats, etc., to improve their appearance. Well-made glaze adheres firmly to the meat. Also used for strengthening soups and sauces.

Glacé, F. Glazed. Anything that is iced or frozen, or anything having a smooth and glossy surface, applied by means of meat glaze, sauce, jelly, or of sugar.

Glacière, F. (Timbre à glace.) Ice box. Refrigerator.

Globe Artichoke. Artichaut, F. A plant extensively cultivated for culinary purposes; like a thistle, with large scaly heads similar to a pine-cone.

Glucose. Molasses. A thick syrupy substance obtained by incompletely hydrolising starch or a starch-containing substance, decolourising and evaporating the product. It is found in various degrees of concentration, ranging from 41 to 45 degrees Baume. An uncrystallisable sugar produced from dextrine, starch, and cellulose by the action of dilute acids and ferments.

Gluten. A sticky substance found in flour. A nitrogenous body present in most cereals; may be obtained by washing flour in a muslin bag under water, when the starch is removed, and the gluten remains. Gluten flour is used mainly for diabetic specialities; it is the albuminous element of the grain, and instrumental as a builder of bodily structures.

Gnocchi, IT. Plural of *gnoccho.* A light savoury dumpling (with a base of potatoes), poached and served with grated cheese and/or a sauce. Also applied to *pâte à choux, i.e., Cnocchi Parisienne,* which, after being passed through a forcer, cut into short lengths and poached, is served with a white sauce, etc. A third type *Gnocchi Romaine,* has a basis of semolina.

71

Godard, F.   Name given to an Entrée of chicken by the inventor, Benjamin Godard, a noted French composer.

Godiveau, F.   Rich veal forcemeat quenelles. Used as a garnish almost exclusively.

Golden Buck.   (*See* BUCK RAREBIT.)

Golden Syrup.   A syrup obtained during the refining of loaf sugar and crystallised "Demerara." It is purer and sweeter than treacle, but thinner in consistency.

Gombaut, Gombo.   (*See* GUMBO.)

Goose. Oie, F.   A favourite dish in autumn and winter; considered at its best at Michaelmas. The goose is an aquatic bird which has long been domesticated in nearly all parts of the world.

Gooseberry. Groseille, F.   The fruit of a prickly shrub indigenous to Great Britain. The Scotch word "grosart" or "groset" is derived from the French name.

Gooseberry Fool.   A half-frozen fruit pulp, served as a sweet. The name is a corruption of "gooseberry foul" (*foulé*), meaning milled or pressed gooseberries. This dish is very popular, but its name is often puzzling, and may be regarded as an example of the degeneration of a foreign kitchen term, a corruption which has destroyed the descriptive meaning. Originally the qualifying adjective was written *foulé* because the stewed gooseberries were crushed and pressed before being mixed with the cream.

Gorgonzola.   An Italian cheese. (*See* CHEESE.)

Gosling. Oison, F.   A young goose.

Gouffé, Jules.   Author of "Le Livre de Cuisine," one of the culinary classics.

Goujon, F.   Gudgeon. Also a term meaning small strips of fish, e.g., sole,—*Goujons de Sole*.

Goulash, Gulyas, Guliàs huis, F.   An Austro-Hungarian dish consisting of beef or veal cut in dice, potatoes, apples, and bacon, seasoned with paprika pepper, served with brown sauce.

Goulu pois or **Pois goulu,** F.   A pea of which the pod is also eaten.

Gourmand, F.   A ravenous eater; a glutton.

Gourmet, F.   An epicure. A judge of good living; one who values and enjoys good eating; a connoisseur of wines.

Goût, F.   Taste or savour. Relish, to perceive by the tongue; the sense of tasting; an intellectual relish.

Goûter, F. An afternoon meal; a meat tea. To taste; to relish.

Graisse, F. Fat, suet, grease.

Granite, F. Granolata. A kind of half-frozen lemon or other fruit water-ice served in glasses.

Grape. Raisin, F. The fruit of the vine. Native of Greece, Asiatic Turkey, and Persia, from whence the vine spread.

Gras, F. Fat, plump. *Gras (au)*. This signifies that the article specified is dressed with rich meat gravy. *Gras-double*—tripe.

Gratin. Baked with encrusted or browned surface; bread-crumbs strewed over meat, fish, macaroni ,cheese, or similar dishes, and browned. *Gratiner*—to brown the surface of the contents of a dish.

Gravy. Jus, F. The juice obtained from meat in cooking, especially from roasts.

Grayling. Ombre, F. The grayling belongs to the same family as the trout. It is found principally in the rivers in the north of England.

Greengage. (*See* REINE-CLAUDE.)

Green Ginger. An excellent fruit preserve which comes to the markets at such reasonable prices that few housekeepers care to preserve their own.

Green Goose. During spring a young goose is so called.

Grenade, F. Pomegranate. The fruit of the pomegranate-tree (grenadier, F.), largely used for preserves, jellies, and syrup.

Grenadine, F., or **Grandine Syrup.** A syrup made from the expressed juice of the pomegranate, and sugar.

Grenadins, F. Small slices of veal (heart shaped), larded and braised.

Grenouille, F. (*See* EDIBLE FROG.)

Grey Mullet. Mulet, Muge, F. (*See* MULLET.)

Grianneau, F. A young grouse.

Griblette, F. Collop of broiled or grilled pork.

Gridiron. Gril, F. A grating placed before or over the fire; used for broiling or grilling. A grill used for broiling over the fire consists of a row of thin steel bars fastened in an iron frame.

Grillade, F. Broiled meat; broiler. *Grillé,* F.—Grilled. A *Mixed grill* consists of a selection of grilled cutlets, bacon, kidney, tomatoes, and sausages.

73

Grilse. A young salmon in its second or third year, after its first return from the sea.

Grimod de la Reynière. Name of a distinguished culinary author and famous gastronome, born 1758, died 1838, author, in 1803, of the famous "Almanach des Gourmands."

Griotte, F. A dark-red cherry, aclled Armenian cherry, suitable for compote and jam.

Griskin of Pork. This joint consists of top of the spare-rib which contains the bones of the spine. In a small pig the griskin and spare-rib are not separated. In some localities it is called "chine of pork."

Grive, F. *(See* FIELDFARE.)

Grivelette. A small thrush from San Domingo.

Grog. A beverage; a mixture of spirits (mostly rum), hot water, and sugar.

Grondin, F. Generic name of many varieties of small fish including gurnard (gournal), roach (rouget), etc.

Groseilles, F. Gooseberries or currants.

Gros-sel, F. Coarse salt.

Grosse-pièce, F. A large joint (of meat or poultry).

Grouse. Coq de bruyère, F. The true, or red grouse (*lagopus scoticus*). Other varieties are the black, or American grouse, the white grouse (usually called the ptarmigan) and the wood grouse or capercailzie, They are chiefly distinguished by having hair-like feathers between their toes, which gives them their name *lagopus*. The sand-grouse, so-called, is not a grouse at all. *(See* SANDGROUSE.) Grouse should be drawn as soon as possible after being killed, as they soon taint; and should be well hung before cooking.

Gruau, F. Gruel, oatmeal; water-gruel.

Gruel. A thin paste generally made of finely-ground oatmeal, but also of barley and other farinaceous food.

Gruyère, F. Name of a Swiss village and valley celebrated for its cheese.

Guava. The guava is a native of the East and West Indies, and grows in South America and China. The fruit is about the size of a hen's egg, yellow or claret in colour, with a thin and brittle rind, which is sometimes stewed in milk, and is also used for making marmalade. The pulp is firm, flesh-coloured, aromatic, sweet, and full of seeds.

Gudgeon. Goujon, F. A small fresh-water fish found in placid streams and lakes, belonging to the carp family. Its flesh is firm and well-flavoured. By the Romans it was served fried at the beginning of supper. The Greeks also held it in some considerable regard.

Guimauve, F.   Marshmallow.

Guinea Fowl. Pintade, F.   The guinea-fowl is a bird of the turkey species, having bluish grey plumage with white dots, and is a little larger than the common fowl. The quality of the flesh is between that of the fowl and the pheasant. It has the advantage of being in season when game is not. This bird is a native of Guiana, not of Guinea.

Guinette, F.   Old name for the guinea-fowl.

Guisado.   A Spanish dish, mostly prepared with meat and potatoes stewed together.

Gulyas.   (*See* GOULASH.)

Gumbo.   Also called Okra. An annual pod of a tree of the hibiscus family. (*Abelmoschus esculentus*) whose green pods, abounding in nutritious mucilage, are much used in the West Indies, etc., for soups and pickles. Chicken gumbo is a purée or soup made fom okra and chicken.

Gurnet or **Gurnard.** Gournal, F.   There are many varieties of this fish—the red, the piper, the streaked, the grey, and the little gurnard. The red gurnet or gurnard is caught in trawls on the west coast of England at all seasons of the year. It is usually about a foot long. It is an excellent fish notwithstanding Falstaff's disparaging allusion to "soused gurnet" in one of Shakespear's plays.

Guyave.   (*See* GUAVA.)

Haché, F.   Minced meat, finely sliced meat. (*See also* HACHIS.)

Hacher-menu, F.   To mince meat finely.

Hachis, F.   Hash. Hashed meat. A favourite from of re-dressing cooked meat. *Salmi di gibier,* F.—hashed game.

Haddock. Aiglefin or merluche, F. Smoked or dried haddock—*merluche fumé,* F. The haddock (*morrhua æglefinus*) is a fish resembling the cod but much smaller, measuring ten to twelve inches in length, and seldom weighing more than two or three pounds. It is distinguished by a dark spot on either side of the body, just beyond the gills. There is a superstition connected with these spots, suggesting that they are marks left by the thumb and forefinger of St. Peter when taking tribute money out of the mouth of a fish of this species. The haddock is found chiefly on the north-east coast; and in winter, migrating in large numbers from these latitudes, it arrives on the coast of Yorkshire. Dried haddock—*Morue fumée* or *salée,* F.

Haggis. Scotch dish. A kind of globular liver sausage, derived from "hag" to chop, or *hachis,* hash. The modern haggis consists of the liver, lights, and heart of a sheep finely chopped, mixed with oatmeal, and suet, and seasoning. This is inserted in a sheep's paunch, and boiled for several hours. Robert Burns immortalised the haggis in a poem. A similar dish was, it is said, a great favourite with the Romans.

Hake. Merluche, F. A kind of sea-fish allied to the cod. (Genus *Merluccius vulgaris.*)

Halaszle. A Hungarian fish stew.

Halbran or **Halebran,** F. (*See* ALBRAN.)

Halibut. Flétan, F. This is one of the largest of the flat fish tribe, specimens five feet long, and weighing from 80 to 100 pounds, being frequently seen in our markets.

Ham. Jambon, F. The hind leg of pork, when it is salted and cured, or smoked.

Hanche, F. Haunch. Name applied to leg and loin part of venison, mutton or lamb.

Hand of Pork. This joint is the fore leg. They are usually salted, boiled, and served either hot or cold. In the North they are called "hamkins."

Hare. Lièvre, F. The hare may be found in most of the northern regions. Unlike the rabbit, which burrows, it makes its home on the surface of the ground, assuming in some measure the same colour as this to avoid detection. Thus we find that in the Polar regions it becomes nearly white in winter, while in summer it turns to a brownish-grey.

76

Hareng, F. Herring. *Hareng fumé,* F.—Bloater. *Hareng mariné,* F.—Pickled herring. (*See* HERRING.)

Harenguets, F. Sprats.

Haricot, F. Bean. Also applied to a thick meat stew, so called from the French word for beans, from which the dish was originally made. (*See* BEANS.) Haricot is also the name of a variety of fat juicy grapes from Cyprus, which have a short season (approx. 6 weeks).

Hash. (*See* HACHIS.)

Hâtelet, F. A small silver skewer garnished with cut roots, truffles, mushrooms, aspic, cocks' combs, etc., used for ornamenting fish and remove dishes.

Hatelette or **Hatelle,** F. Small pieces of meat roasted on a skewer.

Hâtereau, F. Sliced pig's liver, wrapped in pig's caul and cooked on skewers.

Hâtiveau, F. Early pear; name also used for other early fruits.

Hautboy. Caperon, F. A species of strawberry, perfectly white in colour, and of an especially delicate flavour.

Haut goût, F. Fine taste, high flavour, strong seasoning. In Scotland the term means bad or tainted.

Hazel-hen. Gelinotte, F.

Helitherm. The name of a complete programme designed for hospital catering involving special kitchen equipment, conveyor belts and tray service sets.

Hen Turkey. Dinde, F. (*See* also TURKEY.)

Hermitage. A very rich, purple-coloured wine, possessing a special bouquet, generally considered best produced in the South of France.

Herring. Hareng, F. The herring is mostly found in high northern latitudes. They are found in abundance in the North Sea, and are caught off almost every part of the coast of Scotland. Immature herrings, known as "matties," are considered a great delicacy.

Highball. Whisky and soda with ice.

Hind Quarter of Lamb. (*See* QUARTIER D'AGNEAU.)

Hirondelle, F. Swallow.

Hock. The English name for German wines from the Rhine districts.

Hog Pudding. (*See* ANDOUILLE.)

Hollandaise, F. Dutch style, also the name of a rich sauce made from a reduction of vinegar and peppercorns, to which egg yolks and butter are added (a *sabayon* is made).

Homard, F.   Lobster.

Hominy.   A farinaceous food made of maize (Indian corn). It is very nourishing. Derivation from the word "auhuminea," which is the North American Indian term for parched corn.

Honey.   Miel, F.   Sweet juice collected from various flowers by bees. French Narbonne and Swiss honey are both celebrated. The English and Welsh honeys also supply an excellent table delicacy. Honey is said to be one of the most variable of food materials. When pure it is derived solely from the sweet fluid collected from the nectaries of flowers and further elaborated by the honey-bee.

Hongroise, F.   Hungarian.

Hops.   Houblon, F.   The full-grown catkin of a climbing plant employed in the manufacture of beer. It was first introduced into England for cultivation about 1520.

Hop-shoots.   (*See* Jetè d'Houblon.)

Hors-d'Oeuvre, F.   Small side dishes, served cold, generally before the soup, in order to create appetite. They consist of anchovies, oysters, caviare, sardines, dressed cold vegetable of anchovies, oysters, caviare, sardines, dressed cold vegetables, and other dainty relishes.

Horseradish.   Raifort, F.   A species of scurvy-root of peculiarly hot flavour. It forms an excellent relish, stimulating the appetite and promoting digestion. Used grated as a garnish and in sauces.

Hotch-potch (Hochepot).   A soup or stew very popular in Scotland. It is generally made from neck of mutton, and contains a large quantity of peas or barley, with vegetables and meat cut up into dice. It is sometimes a mixture of many things, hence its name.

Hovis Flour and Bread.   Hovis is the registered name for a highly nutritive bread, in the manufacture of which a large proportion of the prepared germ of the wheat is used.

Houblon, F.   (*See* Hops and Jets d'Houblon.)

Huckleberry or Whortleberry.   Airelle Myrtille, F.

Huile, F.   Oil. The oil used for culinary purposes is obtained from the olive-tree. It is used for salad dressing, sauces, for frying, etc. Provence oil and Lucca oil have the highest reputation; the former is, however, considered the best. Cotton-seed oil and groundnut oil is now much used for cheap cooking purposes, though for really good cookery it cannot be recommended.

Huître, F. (*See* OYSTER.)

Huîtres en Coquilles, F. Oysters served in their shells.

Huîtres frites, F. Fried oysters.

Hung Beef. The beef is hung till tender, then salted, rolled tightly in a cloth, and hung up for about three weeks, till it becomes dry. If smoke-dried it will keep for a long time.

Hûre, F. Boar or pig's head; also head and shoulders of some large fish. *Hûre de Sanglier*—wild boar's head.

Ice. Glace, F. (*See* GLACE.)

Iceland Moss, freshly gathered, is boiled and eaten with meat as a vegetable. The jelly made from it when dried makes a nourishing food for invalids.

Ices. Glaces, F. Supposed to have been introduced by Catherine de Medici in the 16th century. Some assert that ice-cream was first invented by a negro, named Jackson, who kept a small confectioner's shop in Soho in the early part of the 18th century.

Icing, E. Glaçure, or Glace, F. A covering for cakes or pastry, made with fine sugar and white of egg, or sugar and water, flavoured and coloured according to taste.

Indienne (à la), F. Indian Style. Generally applied to dishes containing curry or chutney or broth, accompanied with a dish of plain boiled rice.

Irish Coffee. (*See* GAELIC COFFEE.)

Irish Moss. Carregeen. A seaweed which grows in abundance on the coast of Ireland. When cleaned and dried it is used for making jellies; it then forms an excellent dish for invalid dietary.

Irish Stew. A stew of mutton, potatoes, and onions; national dish of Ireland.

Irlandaise (à l'). Irish Style. This term is applied to dishes containing potatoes in some form; these are either introduced during the process of cooking or else served around a dish to form its garnish.

Isinglass. Gelatine, F. The former is prepared from the sound, or swimming bladder, of the sturgeon and other similar fishes. Both isinglass and gelatine are used for giving firmness to liquids, but cannot be regarded as articles of nourishment.

Italienne (à l'), F. Italian Style. With a few exceptions the term implies that the dish is made of entirely or part of macaroni or similar paste, and in which Parmesan cheese or tomato, or both, have been introduced. Garnishing known as *à la Milanaise, à la Napolitaine, à la Parme,* and *à la Florentine* usually contain one or other of the above-named ingredients. A *Sauce Italienne* contains chopped mushrooms and shallots (duxelle) and has a base of *demi-glace.*

Iudabah. Name of an Arab dish. Rice stewed in rich chicken stock and sweetened.

Jacane. A genus of tropical wading birds.

Jacobins. Nickname of quenelles of custard, which became fashionable during the Revolution; after the Restoration their name was changed to Royals.

Jagger or **Jagging-iron.** An implement used for cutting pastry into fancy shapes. It consists of a brass wheel, which is fastened to a handle.

Jalousies. Name given to small puff-paste cakes.

Jam. Confiture, F. A confection or conserve of fruit, made by boiling fruit with sugar to a certain consistency.

Jamaica Pepper. (*See* ALLSPICE.)

Jamaican Coffee. As for French Coffee (*q.v.*) substituting rum for brandy.

Jambon, F. (*See* HAM.) *Jambonneau*—a very small ham.

Jambon froid, F. Cold ham.

Jardinière, F. A mixture of spring vegetables; vegetables stewed down in their own sauce.

Jarret, F. Shin, knuckle. *Jarret de veau*—knuckle of veal.

Jaune-mange, F. A kind of egg-jelly made from gelatine, white wine, lemons, sugar, and eggs. It is so called on account of its yellow colour.

Jean de Carême (John of Lent). A famous cook under Pope Leo X., who received the nickname of "John of Lent" in consequence of a celebrated *soupe maigre* which he used to prepare for his master the Pope. He is supposed to be the direct ancestor of the celebrated Antoine Carême.

Jelly. Gelée, F. Thickened juice of fruits or meats. Concentrated essence of any kind of food, having gelatinous substance. It is obtained by boiling to a glutinous consistence.

Jerked Beef. Beef cut into thin slices and dried in the sun. The word "jerked" is a corruption of the Peruvian word *charqui,* and does not mean that the meat has been shaken.

Jernik-kalwasi. A Russian dish, consisting of semolina, milk, and honey.

Jerusalem Artichoke. Topinambour, F. Originally imported from Brazil. A tuberous root-plant like a white turnip in appearance. It contains about 4 per cent. more water than the potato. It curdles milk like rennet. Used in making Palestine soup, also served as a vegetable, though the word has no connection with Jerusalem, but is a corruption of the Italian *girasol,* the name for the sunflower, which turns with the sun.

Jetée, F. A throw. *Filer de sucre à la jetée*—to spin sugar by throwing.

Jets d'Houblon, F. Hop sprouts. Young sprouts of hops gathered in spring, are cooked and eaten like asparagus.

John Dory. St. Pierre, F. This fish is found in British seas. Its name is supposed to be derived from the French words *jaune dorée* (golden yellow), as its body is marked with yellow. The fish has good flesh, which, strange to say, improves much when about 24 hours have elapsed from the time it was caught.

Johnson, Dr. A noted English gourmand, who had a strong liking for honey and cream.

Joint. Relevé, F. The *grosse-pièce* or *pièce de résistance* of a dinner. On the Continent the joint is usually served after the fish, whilst in this country it is served after the entrées.

Joinville (Prince de). A French nobleman, third son of Louis Philippe I., after whom several dishes are named.

Jordan Almonds. Almonds grown in a garden. "Jordan" is a corruption of the French jardin.

Jugged. Civet, F. A brown stew, of hare or some kind of game, cooked by placing the ingredients in a jar with just sufficient stock or sauce to cover, and then stewing at even temperature in a bainmarie or in the oven.

Julep. Ancient Arabian name for a cooling drink containing mucilage and opium, etc.

Julienne. Name of a vegetable clear soup, first made in 1785 by a noted French chef named Jean Julien, who left his fortune to the poor of Paris. Name also given to a garnish of mixed vegetables cut into very fine shreds.

Jumbles. Under this name pass confections of varying degrees of complication, as the name, signifying confused mixture, seems to indicate.

Junket. Juncate, old English for a cream cheese made in a rush-basket. From Latin *juncus,* a rush. Name of a favourite Devonshire dish, which consists of milk turned with rennet, double cream, sugar, and ground cinnamon or other flavouring. Usually served with fruit, fresh or preserved.

Jus, F. Juice; broth; gravy. The juice of cooked meats seasoned, but without any liaison (thickening).

Jus lié, F. A thickened gravy usually made from brown veal stock.

Kabob. An Indian dish of stewed meat, curried.

Kaffeklatsch, G. Coffee gossips. Name of a German entertainment. Coffee, chocolate flavoured with vanilla and beaten up with egg and cream, all kinds of wafers, cakes, etc., are provided for the guests on such occasions, the company being strictly feminine.

Kagne, F. A sort of vermicelli.

Kail. (*See* KALE.)

Kailcannon. (*See* COLCANNON.)

Kaimak. A Russian sweet, similar to cream custard.

Kaiserfleisch, G. Smoked sucking pig.

Kale, Kail (Scotch). Chou frisé, F. A curly-leaved cabbage. Colewort. In Scotland the term also denotes a vegetable soup containing the vegetables named.

Kangaroo tail soup. A soup similar in flavour to oxtail soup, garnished with thin slices of kangaroo tail.

Kari, F. (*See* CURRY.)

Kebobs (Khubab). Name of a dish served in India and Turkey, consisting of small slices of mutton run on skewers, and grilled or braised.

Kedgeree, Kishri or **Kitchri.** An Indian dish of fish and rice curried. Also a mixture of rice or lentils, cooked with butter, fish, dhall, etc., and flavoured with fennel, onions, spice, etc.

Kelkel. A slice of sole dried and salted.

Ketchup, Catsup. Name of a much-esteemed table sauce. The best known ketchups are made of fresh mushrooms mixed with salt, and flavoured with spices. Tomato ketchup is prepared in a similar way, or walnut ketchup, for which unripe walnuts are used. Word derived from Chinese Kwaitchap.

Kettle of Fish. A kind of fish stew well known in Scotland, locally known as "fish and sauce." It is generally made from haddock.

Kickshaw. Espèce de ragoût or charcuterie, F. This is a name used in cookery which may be given to any dish

83

prepared with extraordinary nicety; but it is usually applied to such things as are regarded as luxuries by the rich. From the French *quelque chose*.

Kid. Chevreau, F. A young wild goat. In the time of our forefathers the flesh was esteemed as much as lamb. The meat is sweet and very tender. It is usually cooked whole, like sucking-pig (larded or barded, and sometimes marinaded).

Kidney. Rognons, F. Sheep's, lamb's, veal, and pork kidneys are alone considered of any account in cookery. They possess a peculiar slightly bitter flavour, which characteristic makes them a favourite dish for breakfast or luncheon. They are best grilled or *sautéd*—(tossed).

King Crab. A crustacean popular in North America, the claws are very large and similar to the lobster in flavour.

Kipper. Name applied to herrings, salmon or mackerel, split open, salted (cured), smoked, and dried. (The word is taken from the Dutch kipper, which means to hatch or to spawn.)

Kirschwasser, Kirsch. A white liqueur distilled from cherries. The best Kirsch comes from the Black Forest, Germany, and from Switzerland.

Kitchen Pepper. A mixture of finely-powdered ginger, cinnamon, black pepper, nutmeg, Jamaica pepper, cloves, and salt. It should be kept in small bottles, closely stoppered.

Kitchener. The ancient name for cook, but now only applied to a kitchen apparatus.

Klösse. German dish, composed of small light forcemeat or dough balls boiled in water, milk, or gravy. These are also made of bread, potatoes, rice, and eggs, and are varied with meat, fish, or liver.

Knödel, G. Bavarian name for a kind of small dumpling.

Knuckle of Veal. Jarret de veau, F. Part below the kneejoint; mostly used for stews and stock.

Kohl-rabi. Chou de Siam. Chou-rave, F. Cabbage turnip. There are three varieties—white, green, and purple. The name is derived from two German words which signify "cabbage-turnip." When young it is very palatable, and extremely wholesome.

Konomoe. Name of a Japanese vegetable.

Koofthas. Name of an Indian dish; a mince of meat or fowl, curried, shaped into balls, and fried.

Koumiss. A beverage originally made by the Tartars from

mare's or camel's milk, fermented. It is made in England by adding yeast to new cow's milk, which, when partially fermented, is kept closely sealed in bottles. It possesses the properties of a gentle effervescent, with the stimulating characteristics derived from the presence of a small quantity of alcohol, while the nutriment of the casein remains unimpaired.

Kourabi. Name of a Swedish sweetmeat, a favourite preparation served with coffee.

Kromeskis. A Polish word, having the same meaning as croquette in French. Balls or rolls of forcemeat or of minced chicken and ham, wrapped in caul, braised or crumbed, or else dipped in batter, and fried.

Krona Pepper. A mild red pepper seasoning of excellent flavour, free from pungency; for kitchen and table use.

Krupnick. Name of a Russian soup.

Kümmel. A German liqueur distilled from caraway seed and coriander.

Lacteal, Lactean. Laiteux, F. Pertaining to milk, milky.

Lactometer. A glass tube for ascertaining the richness of milk or cream.

Lactose or **Milk Sugar.** A sugar or carbohydrate which occurs in the milk of the mammalia.

Ladog, F. Name of a kind of herring found in Lake Ladoga, in Russia, from which it derives its name.

Laflèche, F. A place in France known for its fine quality of capon.

Lagacque. A famous *restaurateur* of the French Revolution, whose establishment was in the garden of the Tuileries.

Lager Beer. The word "lager," as applied to beer, means "stored." It has, however, come to be used as a general term for the light beers brewed in Germany, and other countries, which are for the most part "aged" by other means than cold storage.

Lait, F. Milk. *Lait (au)*—prepared with milk, or in milk. *Lait d'amande*—almond milk, *Petit lait*—whey.

Laitance, F. The soft roe of a fish. Those of herrings, carp or mackerel, are considered a delicacy.

Laitproto. The registered name of a special brand of the casein of milk from which all milk-fat and milk-sugar have been practically eliminated. *Laitproto.* The name of a special brand of milk proteid, prepared from casein, which is practically free from the presence of sugar and fat.

Laitue, F. (*See* LETTUCE.)

Lamb. Agneau, F. A young sheep. Leg of lamb—*gigot d'agneau.*

Lamb's Fry. Animelles, F.

Lambstones. Certain parts taken from young rams to convert them into wethers. They are cooked and served like lamb's sweetbreads, and are considered a delicacy.

Lamprey. Lamproie, F. A species of eel, also called "Nine Eye" on account of having, besides its eyes, seven little holes at the side of its head.

Land o'Cakes. A name sometimes given to Scotland, either because oatmeal cakes are a common national dish, particularly among the poorer classes, or because it is famous for the variety of its cakes, in which it more resembles a continental country than a part of Great Britain.

Landrail or **Corncrake.** A bird of fine flavour, and by some preferred to the partridge. As an article of food, its use is almost entirely confined to the country. It arrives at the beginning of April, and after hatching its eggs leaves at the end of October.

Langouste, F. (*See* CRAWFISH.)

Langue, F. Tongue, E. The tongue of most animals is regarded as a delicacy. The meat is generally juicy and tender; usually cured, then boiled or braised.

Langue de Veau, F. Calf's tongue.

Langues de Chat, F. Very small tea or dessert biscuits (wafers). Literally, cat's tongues, also fine wafers of chocolate.

Languier, F. Smoked hog's or pig's tongue.

Lapereau, F. Young rabbit.

Lapin, F. (*See* RABBIT.)

Lard, Saindoux, F. Pork fat, generally in a refined form. To lard (*larder*) is to pass (*piquer*) a larding pin (*lardoire*), a small strip of bacon or lardoon (*lardon*) through a piece of meat. Larding bacon—*lard à piqués*.

Lard, F. (*See* BACON.)

Lark. Mauviette or Alouette, F. A bird belonging to the finch family. They are caught by means of nets, and are considered a great delicacy.

Laurier, F. (*See* BAYLEAF.)

Lavaret, F. A lake trout which abounds in certain Swiss lakes (Zoug, Constance, etc.), and other lakes in Austria and Bavaria.

Laver. A marine alga or sea-weed, growing on rocks on the sea coasts. It is cooked like spinach, and is served as an accompaniment with roast meat. There are three varieties: the purple, the green, and the sea lettuce. Purple laver is esteemed the best. All are nutritious articles of food, easily digested, and suitable for invalids.

Lax (Norwegian). Lachs, G. Smoked salmon, preserved in oil.

Lazagnes, IT. Thin strips of nouille paste. (*See* NOUILLES.)

Lecithin. A fat which contains phosphorous, found in yolks of eggs.

Leek. Poireau, F. The national symbol or badge of the Welsh. In Scotland it forms, in connection with a boiled fowl, the favourite dish "Cock-a-leekie." Also served as a vegetable, stewed or braised.

Leg. Gigot, F. (*See* CUISSE.)

Légumes, F. Vegetables. Plants used as food.

Le Mans, F. A place in France famous for its poultry, and especially capons.

Lemon. (*See* CITRON, F.)

Lemonade. Limonade, F. A refreshing drink is made of the juice of lemons, the essence of the rind, sugar, and water; sometimes the white of egg and sherry is added, especially if intended as an invalid drink.

Lemon Sole. Limande, F.

Lentil. Lentille, F. The seed of a plant of the same name. In the East, especially in Egypt, they are a staple article of consumtion. Lentils were well known in the ancient world, and are mentioned in the Scriptures as early as the days of Jacob. They are extremely nourishing, but somewhat difficult to digest.

Lettuce. Laitue, F. The lettuce is a cooling, anti-scorbutic, and slightly laxative article of diet. The lettuce has been cultivated in England from a remote age. There are two varieties; the cabbage lettuce, with short open leaves, and the cos lettuce (*romaine*), with longer leaves, which are tied together to blanch.

Levain, F. Leaven, ferment. Dough or batter prepared with yeast before mixing it with the rest of the flour. *Pain sans levain*—unleavened bread. *Levûre*—yeast. A preparation which ferments dough. The froth of beer when it begins to ferment. When pressed and reduced to a dough it preserves a very long time, and is often used in confectionery and as yeast for small bread.

Leveret, Leeraut, Levreteau, F. A young hare.

Liaison, F. The mixture of yolk eggs, cream, etc., used for thickening or binding white soups and sauces. *Lié,* F.— Thickened, bound; applied to creams, soups, and sauces.

Lièvre, F. (*See* HARE.)

Limande, F. (*See* DAB.)

Lime, Limon, F. Is a species of lemon. Smaller and rounder than the ordinary lemon (*citron*); the lime tree is a native of Asia. The juice of this fruit is imported into England in large quantities for the manufacture of citric acid. (*See* CITRIC ACID.)

Limpet. Limpets are found on the sea-shore adhering tightly to the rock. They have only one shell, and are prepared for table like cockles and other bivalves.

Ling. Lingue, F. A fish of the same species as hake. It is a native of the northern seas—the Orkneys, the Yorkshire and Cornish coasts, as well as off the Scilly Islands. In form it resembles the cod, but it is more slender.

Liqueur, F. Liquor. A liquid cordial, such as Maraschino, Curacao, Kümmel, Chartreuse, Bénédictine, etc.

Lit, F. Bed. Thin slices of meat or vegetables spread in layers used for culinary purposes.

Liver. Foie, F.

Lobscouse. A stew of beef or mutton. Potatoes, onions, bones, etc., are boiled until the potatoes are nearly done, then the minced meat is added, when the cooking is continued until the meat is ready.

Lobster. Homard, F. The lobster belongs to the crab tribe, the second great division of Crustaceæ. It is highly esteemed as an article of food, being very palatable and supposed to possess great nutritive qualities, yet many people consider it somewhat indigestible. The chief supply comes from Norway where the fish is very abundant. Nearly all the rocky coasts of Great Britain supply a tolerable quantity of lobsters.

Loin. Longe, F. The back portion nearest the leg of an animal. *Longe de veau*—loin of veal.

Long Pepper. This spice, very similar in taste and smell to ordinary pepper, is much used in making curry-powder and pickles.

Lorgnette, F. Fried onion rings; name also applied to small dessert biscuits and candied fruit.

Lotte or **Burbot,** F. Eel-pout, burbot. The viviparous blenny. A fresh-water fish, very often taken for the ordinary eel; prepared like eels or lampreys.

Louis XIV. A French monarch in whose reign Epicureanism began to flourish. He introduced it, and used both liqueurs and pears.

Louis XV. A French monarch as well as an epicure, who decorated Madam du Barri's female cook.

Louis XVI. An epicure in whose reign *restaurateurs* first became professional men. He introduced the potato, first as a flower, then as a food.

Louis XVIII. Reintroduced gastronomy as a fine art after the Revolution. Was himself a cook, who. it is said, invented *Truffes à la purée d'ortolans*.

Lucine, F. Clam. *Lucines papillons*—soft clams.

Lucullus. Name of the famous Roman epicure and field-marshal, Lucius Licinius Lucullus, 114–57 B.C. Said to have once given a banquet costing £20,000.

Lunch. Déjeuner à la fourchette, F. A repast between breakfast and dinner. Luncheon is claimed to be derived from the old English word "lunch," meaning a lump. The modern meal is a very different matter from the original "lunch," which was a mere snack between meals. In the 16th century a "lunch of bacon" meant merely a slice or hunk of it. Burns, in his "Holy Fair," says: "An' cheese an' bread, frae women's laps, was dealt about in lunches."

Luting. A paste used for fastening lids on pie-dishes in which game or other preserve is potted.

Luzinzeth, an Arab sweet cake. Almond cakes; they consist of thin shells of pastry containing a rich almond stuffing and a delicately-flavoured cream; they are served in sauce of sweet melted butter, and form a delicacy.

Lyonnaise (à la), F. Lyons Style. As a garnish it generally signifies that shredded onion (fried) has been introduced as one of the principal ingredients.

Macaroni. Maccaroni, IT. This is a peculiar paste prepared from flour and manufactured into tubes. It is an Italian invention. The name is said to be taken from a Greek derivation, meaning the blessed bread, in allusion to the ancient custom of eating it at feasts for the dead.

Macaroons. A kind of sweet biscuit made of almonds, sugar, and the white of eggs.

Mace. Arille, F. A spice which grows as a sort of leafy network, enveloping the nutmeg—has a more delicate flavour that the nutmeg. The tree is a native of the Molucca Islands (Indian Ocean), but is also successfully cultivated in Indonesia, Mauritius, and Trinidad (West Indies).

Macédoine, F. A mixture of various kinds of vegetables or fruits, cut in even-shaped discs. The name is also applied to a collection of ripe fruit embedded in jelly and set in a mould, or a fruit salad flavoured with liqueurs and syrup.

Macéré, F. Steeped, macerated, or soused.

Mâche, F. Lamb's lettuce; corn or field salad.

Mackerel. Maquereau, F. A fish. Name derived from the Latin macularelli (little spots). Mackerel contain a larger proportion of fatty matter than many other kinds of fish, and therefore lose their freshness more quickly. They are nutritious, delicate in flavour, but less easily digested than fish possessing less fatty matter. They are a migratory fish. In the winter they retire to deep waters, but during summer they are caught in large numbers near the coast, and the best are caught in the English Channel.

Macon. A town in Burgundy, France, renowned for its Burgundy wines.

Macoquer or **Calebasse,** F. Fruit of the calabash-tree (*calebassier*), grown in America. The fruit resembles the melon, and has an agreeable taste.

Macreuse, F. Widgeon. A black water-fowl of the wild duck tribe.

Madeleine, F. A particular kind of small cake, well known throughout France.

Madère, F. Madeira wine. A Spanish wine, very often used in cooking, especially in sauces.

Madras. Generally applied to a dish flavoured with curry or chutney.

Maigre (au), F. Soups and dishes made without meat. Applied to Lenten and fast-day dishes.

Maintenon, F. Name of the Marchioness Francoise d'Aubigné; born 1635, died 1719; a great patroness of cooks, a born admirer of fine cooking. Several dishes are called *à la Maintenon*. The dish *Côtelettes de veau à la Maintenon* is said to have been invented by this lady, who was Louis XIV.'s favourite, and did all in her power to tempt the failing appetite of the king when he was advanced in age.

Maïs, F. (*See* MAIZE.)

Maitrank, G. (May drink). A delicious beverage, originally consumed in Germany—made of hock or other white wine, which is flavoured with woodruff, lemon, bay leaves, and sugar.

Maître d'Hôtel (à la), F. Hotel steward's fashion. Also the name of a flavouring butter, mixed with chopped parsley and seasoned with lemon-juice, pepper, and salt. Served on grilled meats. *Maître d'hôtel* sauce is a white sauce containing chopped parsley. Dishes surnamed *à la Maître d'hôtel* generally signify quickly and plainly prepared food in which parsley is used as the principal flavouring.

Maize. Maïs, F. Indian or Turkey corn. A complete food containing a large proportion of fat in addition to nitrogenous and mineral elements. (*See also* CORNFLOUR.)

Malaga. An amber-coloured wine produced in the Malaga district in Spain.

Malart or **Malard,** F. Mallard, the common wild drake.

Malmsey. A wine largely consumed in the Middle Ages. It

91

is imported from Sardinia, Sicily, Madeira, and the Canary Islands.

Malt. Barley or other grain steeped in water until it germinates, then dried in a kiln for use in brewing.

Maltose. Malt sugar, produced by action of malt on starch.

Mamaliga. A national dish of Roumania; a porridge-like preparation of corn, meal, and sheep-milk cheese.

Mammée. The fruit of the mammée-tree, of the apple species, which grows in tropical America.

Mandarine, F. Mandarin orange.

Mange-tout, F. Name of a variety of sweet peas, wax, and butter beans, of which the pod is also eaten.

Mangle, F. The fruit of the mangrove.

Mango. Mangue, F. A fruit about the size of a large pear. It is eaten just as gathered from the tree, or boiled, or as a sweet salad. It is also made into preserve and chutney. The best mangoes are grown in the Bombay districts. Several preparations are produced from this fruit, mango chutney and mango pickle being the best known in this country. Mango jelly is a very favourite table condiment in India, also a kind of a sweetmeat called amont; the dried shreds of green mangoes are known as am-chool; the latter is a pleasantly flavoured condiment used extensively in the preparation of Indian dishes.

Manié, F. Kneaded; mixed with the hands. *Beurre manié*— equal parts of butter and flour mixed together.

Manioc. A tropical plant, from which tapioca and cassava are taken.

Maquereau, F. (*See* MACKEREL.)

Maquereau grillé Maître d'Hôtel. Grilled mackerel with parsley butter.

Marabout, F. A very large coffee-pot.

Maraschino, IT. Marasquin, F. A deliciously flavoured white liqueur prepared from wild cherries, raspberry and cherry stones, used for flavouring jellies, ices, etc.

Marbré, F. Marbled. Word used in connection with certain cakes and gelatine dishes.

Marcassin, F. Grice; a wild boar under a year old; generally cooked whole.

Marengo. An Italian village, which gives its name to the dish *Poulet sauté à la Marengo*. The dish is said to have first been served to Napoleon I. by his chef, who hurriedly prepared a fowl in this fashion after a battle.

Marennes, F.   Place on the south-western coast of France, whence come the famous Marennes oysters.

Margarine.   The name given by Act of Parliament to imitation butters formerly called butterine. "Margarine" means "pearly," the original margarine having been a substance isolated from fats by the great French chemist, Michel Eugène Chevreul, who named it in admiration of the pretty pearl-like crystals in which he obtained it. Thus margarine is a sister etymologically of all the Margarets, their common parent being the Greek word for a pearl, which was of Oriental origin. It is so-called mainly because the law found that "butterine" sounded so much like "butter" that customers might be imposed upon.

Margot, F.   Magpie.

Marguéry, F.   Name of a famous Paris restaurateur. The inventor of the dish known as *filet de sole à la Marguéry*.

Marie-Louise.   Second wife of Napoleon I., born 1791, died 1847. The lady was a great gourmand in her time.

Marigold.   A flavouring herb, also known as Pot Marigold. It is a native of Spain, and was introduced into England in 1573.

Marinade, F.   The brine in which fish or meat is soused or pickled, before cooking.

Mariné, F.   Pickled, cured, *Marinière*—mariner style.

Marjolaine, F.   Marjoram. An excellent kitchen herb of strong flavour, used fresh or dried for game seasoning; also for flavouring sauces, forcemeat, etc. There are several varieties, all of an agreeable aromatic flavour. The sweet or knotted marjoram is a native of Portugal.

Mark or **Marquer,** F.   To prepare meats, etc., for braising, roasting, or stewing.

Marmelade, F.   Marmalade. The term "marmalade" originated in Portugal. In that country marmalade was generally made from oranges, but sometimes quinces were used. Extending this view certain dictionaries define marmalade as being made from any kind of sour fruit. Apple and lemon marmalades are well-known table conserves.

Marmite, F.   The stock-pot. A copper, iron or earthenware vessel used for making stock. Originally a French iron pot used for *Pot au feu* and similar soups. *Petits Marmite,* F.—A popular French soup served in little earthen casseroles. *Marmite à Vapeur*—steam-kettle. This name is also given to a valuable food extract used largely for soups, gravies and stews. Marmite is claimed to be the invention of Papin, who is said to be the discoverer of steam, and who introduced his marmite into London in 1675.

Marquer, F. To prepare, and arrange in a stewpan or braising pan, a piece of meat ready for cooking.

Marrons, P. Large chestnuts. (*See* also under CHESTNUT.)

Marrons glacés, F. Candied, glazed or sugar-dipped chestnuts.

Marrowbone. Os à moëlle, F. The large hollow bones of animals, which contain a fatty substance called marrow.

Marsala. A wine in some respects resembling sherry and Madeira, so named after Marsala, in the Island of Sicily, near to which the grapes are grown.

Martin-sec, F. A winter pear, much used for cooking purposes.

Maryland. Applies to a method of preparing chicken *Suprême de volaille Maryland.* The wing of the chicken is egg and breadcrumbed, shallow fried and garnished with banana fritter, sweetcorn and bacon.

Marzipan or **Marchpane.** Almond paste. Delicate German dessert dainties made from almond paste. Name is said to be derived from *Marci Panis*—bread of St. Mark.

Mask. Masquer, F. To cover or coat any kind of cooked meat with rich gravy or savoury jelly. To sauce a dish which is ready for serving; also to mask the inside of a mould with savoury jelly or *chaudfroid* sauce when required for entrées.

Maté, F. A Paraguayan tea, commonly called Maté, the real name being Yerba de Maté; it consists of the powdered leaves and green shoots of plants; well known to the native Indians of South America.

Matelote, F. A rich brown fish stew with wine and herb flavouring. Usually prepared from freshwater fish—carp, tench, pike, eel, etc.

Matignon, F. The name given to a preparation of vegetables, (carrots, celery and onions) stewed in butter with thyme, bayleaf and Madeira wine; used in a number of different dishes.

94

Matzoth or **Motza.**   Large and very thin unleavened biscuits eaten during the Jewish passover.

Mauve, F.   Gull.

Mauviette, F.   Common name for a fatted lark (*Alouette*).

Mavrodaphne.   A Greek liqueur.

May Drink.   A beverage of the type and character of white wine cup flavoured with May flowers. It is of German origin, where it is largely consumed during the spring.

Mayonnaise, F.   A kind of salad of fish or poultry, with a thick cold sauce made of yolks of eggs, oil, and vinegar; a salad sauce or dressing. The sauce is said to have been invented by the chef to the Duc of Richelieu, after the victory of Mahon (*Mahonnaise*).

Mazagran, F.   A glass of black coffee, sugar, and iced water.

Mazarin, F.   A small almond cake, named after Cardinal Mazarin, the French statesman, who, it is claimed, introduced chocolate into Europe.

Mazarines.   Turbans. Forcemeat ornaments of fish, poultry or game.

Mead.   A fermented liquor composed of honey and water; a sweet drink. The word "honeymoon" is derived from the old English custom of drinking mead as a special beverage for thirty days after the wedding feast.

Meat.   Viande, F.

Macque (Pain de la).   French pastry, something made like cream puffs.

Médaillion, F.   Medallion. A name applied to round fillets, meat preparations, etc., in a round form.

Mediants, F.   Name given to four different kinds of dried dessert fruit; almonds, filberts, figs, and dried Malaga grapes.

Medlar.   Nèfle, F.   A fruit about the size of very small apples. It is harsh to the taste, even when ripe. The tree on which the medlar grows is a native of Europe and the temperate climes of Asia. It has long been cultivated in this country.

Melaine, F.   A colouring matter.

Mélange, F.   Mixture. *Mélangé*—mixed. *Melé*—mixed.

Mela Stregata, IT.   A crisp chocolate shell filled with dairy icecream flavoured with Strega liquer.

Melettes, F.   Sprats. A useful little fish.

Melisse, F.   Balm-mint.

Melon.   Mélon, F.   A plant and fruit of the same genus as the cucumber. First imported into England from Jamaica. Melons are very extensively cultivated in Egypt and India, and in all the tropical regions. A greatly esteemed dessert fruit.

Melongena. (*See* AUEBRGINE.)

Melone proscuitto, IT. A portion of melon garnished with a slice of Parma ham.

Melted Butter. Beurre fondu, F. The former name stands also for a plain white sauce, described by the French as the one English sauce.

Menthe, F. (*See* MINT.). *Crème de Menthe*—a liqueur of peppermint flavour.

Menu, F. The bill of fare. Literally the word means minute detail of courses. A list of the dishes which are to be served at a meal. Menus were first used in 1541. Pronounce "menu" as "meh-neu" so that the second syllable is sounded as something between "new" and "neuo." *Menus droits*—pig's ears served as an entrée. *Menu-gibier.* F.—Small game, such as partridges, grouse, pheasants, etc. *Menu rôti,* F.—Small roast birds.

Méringue, F. Light pastry, made of white of eggs and sugar filled with cream custard or ice. *Méringué*—frosted.

Merise, F. A wild cherry. *Merisier*—wild cherry-tree. Kirschwasser is made of this fruit.

Merlan, F. Whiting. A delicate fish allied to the cod.

Merle, F. Blackbird.

Merluche, F. Haddock. The term *merluche* is also loosely applied to hake, and to haddock, cod, and hake when dried. (*See Aiglefin.*)

Merry-thought. A forked bone in the breast of a chicken. Probably a corruption of the word "marry", from a custom among young people in olden times, when two persons held one fork of the bone each, and then pulling it in half, supposing that, by some oracular influence, the one obtaining the larger half of the bone would be the first to marry.

Merveille, F. Name applied to a kind of small cake.

Mess. A dish of food. A number of persons who cater or eat together.

Mets, F. The meal, or dish. *Mets de farine*—farinaceous. *Entremets de douceur*—sweets.

Metternich (Prince). An Austrian statesman, after whom several dishes are named. (1773-1859)

Mexicaine, F.   Mexican style. Garnishes so termed usually include tomatoes, pimentoes, mushrooms and sometimes eggplants.

Miche, F.   Loaf. *Miche de pain*—loaf of bread, etc. *Mie de pain,* F.—Soft bread; crumbs.

Microwave oven.   In this oven electro magnetic waves are produced by a magnetron. When food is placed in a microwave field it quickly becomes hot as it absorbs energy from the microwaves. This energy is transferred into heat within the substance itself by a molecular friction effect.

Middlings.   The coarser part of flour. A common kind of flour.

Miel, F.   (*See* HONEY.)

Miette, F.   Crumb of bread.

Mignardises, F.   Small dainty dishes.

Mignonette Pepper.   Coarsely-ground white peppercorns which resemble mignonette seed.

Mignon, F.   Name applied to very small portions of fillets, *filet mignon,* etc.

Mignonne, F.   A kind of peach, and a variety of pear.

Mignot, F.   A cheese made in Normandy.

Mijoter, F.   To cook slowly; to simmer gently over a small fire.

Milanaise, F.   A name given to certain dishes which contain macaroni, cheese, and nearly always tomato. Also the name of small dessert biscuits.

Milk. Lait, F.   (*See* LAIT.)

Millecanton, F.   Name of a small fish of the whitebait kind, found in the Lake of Geneva; cooked in the same manner as whitebait. In season in July and August.

Millefeuille, F.   Thousand leaves. Milfoil. A cake made of several layers of puff pastry, one on top of the other, interlaid with jam, etc.

Millet.   A plant and its grain; indigenous to tropical countries; there are several varieties, of which India provides the best.

Mincemeat.   Meat chopped very fine. This name is also given to a mixture consisting of finely-minced suet and raisins, sugar, currants, spices, sometimes cooked meat, and brandy. Used for a favourite kind of small pastry known as a mince pie.

Mince pies.   Small pastry patties filled with mincemeat. Traditionally eaten in England at Christmas.

Minestra. An Italian vegetable soup with rice and cheese.

Minnow. Veron, F. A very small fresh-water fish.

Mint. Menthe, F. A small aromatic plant believed to be indigenous to Great Britain, where it has been known since Saxon times.

Mint Julep. Name of an American drink.

Minute, à la, F. A surname given to dishes which are hurriedly prepared; or anything cooked in the quickest possible style. Omelets and grills come under this heading.

Mirabeau, F. A French revolutionist, son of the Marquis de Mirabeau. A rich sauce, and a few dishes, whose garnish includes anchovies and olives, are named after him.

Mirabelle, F. A kind of small yellow plum of exquisite flavour, it is a cross between a greengage and a very luscious plum, but much smaller. The fruit is very sweet and juicy. It is used for compotes, fresh or dried.

Mirepoix, F. The foundation preparation of vegetables, herbs, and bacon, for brown soups and sauces; also for braised meats, etc. Name said to be derived from the Duc de Mirepoix.

Mirliton, F. A kind of French pastry. Tartlets with a basis of puff-paste and filled with a custard mixture.

Miroton, F. Thin slices of cooked meat, usually beef, re-heated in an Espagnole sauce, with onions.

Mirtilles, F. (*See* MYRTILLE.)

Mitonner, F. To steep and allow to boil during a certain time.

Mock Turtle Soup. Potage de tete de veau, or fausse tortue, F.

Moëlle de Bœuf, F. Beef marrow. The fatty substance in the hollow part of bones.

Moka, F. Mocha. A fine quality of coffee, which, however, does not exclusively come from Mocha, as it is mostly produced in Mysore. *Crème de Moka*—a liqueur of Mocha flavour.

Mollet, F. Soft. *Oeufs mollets*—lightly-boiled eggs.

Mont d'Or, F. Name of an excellent Swiss white wine; also a French cheese.

Mont-frigoul, F. A soup in which semolina forms the chief ingredient.

Montglas, F. A French writer of note, after whom several dishes are named. Properly Mont-glat.

Montgolfier, Filet à la. Invention of the first aeronauts, fillets being blown out and distended in balloon fashion.

Montmorency, F. A bitter cherry.

Montpellier, F. Savoury herb butter. A French city renowned for its many culinary specialities.

Morel. Morille, F. A fungus found in woods and orchards. It is said to possess great stimulating properties; used as garniture for fricassées, and for soups and sauces.

Morello. A variety of dark red cherry used in many dishes as a garnish, or for such dishes as *Cerises flambées*.

Morillon, F. A black grape; also name of a blue-winged duck.

Mortadelle, F. Mortadella, IT. A kind of sausage largely manufactured in Bologna (Italy).

Mortifié, F. Term applied to meat and game well hung.

Morue, F. Codfish. (*See* CABILLAUD and MERLUCHE.)

Moscovien, F. Muscovite. Moscow Style.

Mote or **Moti.** Name of an Indian fish curry.

Motza. (*See* MATZOTH.)

Mouille bouche, F. Bergamot pear.

Mouiller, F. To add broth, water, or any other suitable liquid, during the cooking of meats. *Mouillette,* F. Toast dipped in liquid.

Moule, F. Mould. Also mussel (*q.v.*).

Mousse, F. A light ice-cream. Among the definitions given for the word are: mossy, froth, and foam. *Mousse frappée* is a dish prepared with whipped cream and flavouring, frozen without working. Hot puddings are also prepared as mousses; also applied to other dishes made of the soufflé type. *Moussé*—frothy.

Mousseline Sauce. A froth-like sauce, usually made of hollandaise (fish stock, butter, egg-yolks, etc.) and whipped cream. Other mousseline sauces are made with tomato or spinach flavouring.

Mousseron, F. A kind of white mushroom, principally used for ragoûts.

Moutarde, F. Mustard, the seeds of a plant, Sinapis nigra (*black*) and Sinapis alba (*white* or *yellow*). A pungent pulverised seed, chiefly used as a relish or condiment. English mustard was first manufactured at Durham in 1729. The recipe was kept a secret for many years. Some traditions assert that a lady named Clements, of Durham, first introduced mustard as a condiment in 1720.

Mouton, F. Mutton. Sheep. South Down mutton—*Pré-salé,* F. Leg of mutton—*Gigot de mouton,* F.

Muffins. Light, spongy cakes baked on an iron plate over the fire. Generally toasted and eaten at tea, but in the market-places of many northern towns they are sold slit in halves, with slices of ham inserted, thus forming a very substantial sandwich.

Mufle de Bœuf, F. Ox cheek.

Mulberry. Mûre, F. The fruit of a tree bearing the same name. They are preserved, and also made into wine. The leaves of the mulberry are the principal food of the silkworm, and for this purpose the tree is largely cultivated in warm climates.

Mullet. Rouget, F. A fish. There are two varieties, red and grey, but the first-named is more highly esteemed. The striped red mullet was much esteemed by the ancients, especially the Romans.

Mull (to), practically means to heat up, sweeten and spice drinks, particularly wine, such as sherry or claret, etc.

Mulligatawny. An Indian curry soup; a paste made of curry; derives its name from two Tamil words, *molegoo* (pepper) and *tunnee* (water).

Mumbled Hare. Minced cooked hare's meat, flavoured, spiced, and acidulated, put into a stewpan with beaten eggs and butter, and cooked to consistency by constant stirring.

Mûre, F. (*See* MULBERRY.)

Mûre de Ronce, Mûre sauvage, F. (*See* BLACKBERRY.)

Muscade (Noix de), F. Nutmeg. (*See* NUTMEG.)

Muscadelle, F. Musk pear.

Muscat. F. Muscadine. A white grape (muscadine grape).

Muscovado. Name given to unrefined sugar.

Mushroom. Champignon, F. There are twenty-nine varieties of the edible mushroom, and one of the most beautiful of the British varieties is the red-fleshed mushroom, generally abundant in all woody places, and known by its brown top, white gills, and perfect ring encircling the bulbous stem. The most popular species is the meadow mushroom. In England mushrooms are used principally as a flavouring for made dishes, but in Russia, Poland, and some parts of Germany, they are used more extensively as an article of food. The toadstools, the poisonous varieties, are usually distinguished by their fœtid odour. (*See also* Cèpe.)

Mussel. Moule, F. A variety of shell-fish. They inhabit two black shells, and should be boiled in them as soon as possible after being caught. When deprived of their beard, as it is called, they may be fried, scalloped or stewed, and eaten without injurious effects unless the mussels have fed on sewage or other contaminating matter. They are very common on all the English coasts, and are especially plentiful at the mouth of the Mersey.

Mustard. (*See* Moutarde.)

Myrtille. Bilberry. A fruit used for compotes, syrups, and sweet sauces.

Naartje. Cape orange, about the size of the Mandarin.

Napolitaine (à la), F. Naples or Neapolitan Style. Often applied to various dishes, notably a tri-coloured ice made in brick form. It also applies to dishes garnished with spaghetti bound with tomato sauce and parmesan cheese.

Nappe, F. Table-cloth. *Nappé,* F.—To lightly cover, mask, or coat anything with sauce or jelly; to dip, as in fondants, etc.

Nasturtium. Capucine, F. Indian cress. A native plant of Peru, lately acclimatised in Great Britain, the seeds of which have a pungent taste, not unlike capers. The leaves and flowers of this plant have valuable dietetic properties, and make a pleasant addition to salads.

Natives. An English term for oysters, particularly those spawned and bred on the English Coasts, notably Essex and Kent.

Naturel (au), F. Uncooked, or boiled in water. Plain, simple; plainly and quickly prepared.

Nau de Morue, F. Cod sounds.

Navarin, F. A stew of mutton or lamb. A kind of haricot mutton. The name is of ancient origin, being mentioned in one of the plays of Sodelle in the early part of the 17th century. Turnips form the principal garniture of a navarin.

Navet, F. Turnip, E. A bulbous root used for soups, as a vegetable, and for flavouring. *Navette*—wild turnip.

Neat's Foot. The foot of a calf or ox.

Neat's Tongue. The tongue of a calf or ox.

Néctarine, F. Nectarine peach. A variety of peach, but, unlike the peach, it has a smooth skin.

Nèfle, F. (*See* MEDLAR.)

Negus. Name of a hot drink composed of port wine, sugar, nutmeg, and lemon-juice; so-called after Colonel Negus (in the reign of Queen Anne).

Neige, F. Snow. Whites of egg beaten to snow or stiff froth.

Nepaul Pepper. A yellowish pepper of the same character as cayenne and Guinea pepper, but not so hot, being a species of capsicum of a sweet, pungent flavour. It is largely grown in Hindustan.

Néroli. Orange flower essence.

Nesselrode. Name of a pudding, iced, flavoured with chestnuts, invented by Mony, chef to the famous Count Nesselrode. The name Nesselrode usually indicates the presence of chestnuts.

Neufchâtel. A soft cream-like kind of Swiss cheese.

Newburg, F. The name describes a method of preparing lobster, *Homard Newburg,* in which a rich lobster sauce is employed made from cream and egg yolks and flavoured with sherry or madeira, *Homard Newburg* can be made using raw lobsters or made from cooked lobster.

Newtown Pippins. A variety of apples of excellent flavour, originally from Devonshire, and taken across the Atlantic two centuries ago. In the interval attempts have been made to cultivate the Newtown here for market purposes, but the fruit then loses its rich, aromatic flavour. It is named after Newtown, on Long Island, U.S.A.

Nids. Nests. *Nids d'hirondelles de Chine*—Chinese birds' nests. (*See* BIRDS' NESTS.)

Nightcap. Popular name given to grog, mulled wine or beer, or other hot drink, taken just before going to bed.

Niokes or **Niokies.** A farinaceous dish, prepared with semolina or Indian maize, flavoured with grated cheese, cream, etc. Of Russian invention.

Nitrogen. A most important element of the atmosphere as it forms approx. ⅘ of its volume; it enters into the composition of many of the substances used as food, essential to plant and animal life.

Niverolle, F. Snowbird.

Nivette, F. A kind of peach.

Noce, F. Wedding. *Diner de Noce*—wedding feast. *Déjeuner de Noce*—wedding breakfast. *Gâteau de noce*—wedding-cake.

Noisette, F. Hazel-nut. Also name of small round pieces of lean meat, such as lamb or mutton cutlets with bone and fat removed. *Noisette* in cookery also means a small nut or kernel, or the part from the middle, hence the noisette of beef tenderloin is a slice cut from the centre.

Noix, F. Walnut. *Noix de Brésil*—Brazil nuts, *Noix de coco*—coconut.

Noix de Muscat, F. (*See* NUTMEG.)

Noix de Veau, F. Cushion of veal or kernel of veal.

Nonnat, F. A small fish, similar to whitebait.

Nonnettes, F. Small anis-flavoured cakes.

Nonpareilles, F. A French candy or *bon-bons*.

Noques, F. Small dumplings made from flour, cheese, milk, or cream, boiled in stock or salt water, and served as a dish or as garnish, also called Niokis.

Norfolk Dumplings. Often called drop dumplings or spoon dumplings, because the batter, made of milk, flour, eggs, etc., is dropped into boiling water from a spoon.

Normande (à la), F. Normandy Style. The name implies that the flavour of apple has been introduced into the composition of the dish, with the exception of a dish known as *filets de soles à la Normande,* and other fish entrées.

Norvégienne, F. Norwegian. Applies to a method of preparing cold fish especially lobster, spiny lobster or salmon. Also describes certain sweet dishes many of which include meringue.

Nougat, F. Almond rock candy. A sweetmeat made with sugar, honey, almonds, pistachios, and other nuts.

Nouilles, F. Nudeln, G. Noodles. A very useful paste preparation. It consists of a stiff dough made with flour and eggs, rolled out very thinly, cut up in thin strips and boiled.

Often served as garnish or fried; can also be served as sweet savoury.

Nourrir, F. Culinary meaning, to enrich, by adding butter, cream, oil, etc., to other ingredients.

Noyau, F. The stone of a fruit; a liqueur flavoured with peach or nectarine kernels.

Nudeln, G. (*See* NOUILLEÈ.)

Nutmeg. Noix de Muscade, F. The nutmeg known in commerce is the seed of the *Myristica Moschata,* a native of the Molucca Islands, but cultivated in Java, Sumatra, Cayenne, and some of the West Indian Islands. The fruit, when separated, exposes the kernel (the nutmeg) enveloped by a network of mace (*q.v.*).

Oatmeal. Gruau d'avoine, F. The grain of the oat dried in a kiln and ground. There are three kinds: coarse, medium, and fine. Oatmeal when cooked is considered a fair example of a complete food. Generally eaten in the form of porridge of gruel.

Oats. Avoine, F. Oats contain all the nutrient properties, although not in so well balanced proportions as are found in wheat.

Œuf, F. Egg. *Blanc d'œuf*—white of egg. *Jaune d'œuf*—yolk of egg. *Œufs durs*—hard-boiled eggs. *Œufs mollets*—soft-boiled eggs. *Œufs brouillés*—scrambled eggs. *Œufs frits*—fried eggs. *Œufs à la coque*—boiled eggs.

Œufs farcis, F. Stuffed eggs.

Œufs pochés, F. Poached eggs.

Ogen. A variety of melon similar to the Charentais, (*q.v.*) but usually larger in size; grown in Israel.

Oie, F. (*See* GOOSE.)

Oignon, F. Onion. A vegetable plant of the allium family; a valuable culinary adjunct for flavouring and garnishing purposes. Onion soup (*soupe à l'oignon*), or onion porridge, is regarded as an excellent restorative in debility of the digestive organs. (*See also* ONION.)

Oiseau, F. Bird.

Oison, F. Gosling; young goose.

Okra. Orchra. (*See* GUMBO.)

Okroschka. A Russian national soup.

Old Fashioned. A popular American cocktail, consisting of rye whiskey or bourbon with sugar syrup, angostura bitters and ice; decorated with a twist of lemon peel, and thin slice of orange and a maraschino cherry.

Olive, F. Olive. Fruit of the olive-tree, used as *hors d'œuvre,* and as garnish for sauces, stews, salads, etc. There are several varieties: Italian, French, Greek and Spanish. Those imported from Spain are the largest and most esteemed.

Olive Oil. Huile d'Olive, F. Made from ripe olives, which are dark purple in colour, like a damson plum. The finest quality of this comes from the fruit that has just begun to ripen, but this does not yield nearly so much oil. The pulp of the fully ripe fruit gives 70 per cent. of oil. The finest quality has a pale greenish tint, a pleasant smell, and a faintly pungent taste. It is chiefly exported from Italy and the south of France.

Olives (Meat). Small rolls of meat enclosing forcemeat, usually braised.

Olla Podrida. Spanish national dish, prepared with different sorts of meat, sausages, and vegetables.

Oloroso. Term applied to sherry from its 14th to 20th year.

Omble or **Omble Chevalier,** F. An excellent freshwater fish of the salmon tribe, found in the Lake of Geneva and other Swiss lakes and rivers, weighing up to 15 lbs.; in season during January and February. This fish (*salmo salvellinus*) is of the true salmon family and is not be to confused with the grayling, *Ombre*. (*See below*).

Ombre, F. Grayling. A fresh-water fish, resembling a trout. Its flesh has a flavour of thyme, hence its Latin name *thymallus*. It is a distinct family from the salmon and is not to be confounded with *Omble*. (*See aboêe*.)

Omelette, F. Omelet. A cushion-shaped preparation of eggs. A pancake or fritter of eggs, etc. Its name is supposed to be derived from the word *œufs mélés*.

Onion. Oignon, F. A plant of the onion tribe, the leek, shallot, and garlic being of the same species. After salt, the onion is the most valuable seasoning in cookery; it possesses stimulating and digestive properties.

Orange. This well-known fruit is principally imported from Sicily, Spain, Portugal, and Malta. The Seville orange is used for making marmalade. So far as history authentically knows the orange originated in India and China, and was carried by the Arabs to Syria, Africa, and Spain. In Sanscrit it has been called "nagrungo," in Arabic "narang," in Spanish "naranja," and in Italian "arancia." Our "orange" comes from the Provençal. From Spain the orange came to America, and it was first found in Mexico. In California it was introduced by the Spanish padres, who planted trees near the missions of Southern California. These formed the basis of the great Californian orchards of to-day.

Orangeade. A drink made of orange-juice.

Orangeat, F. Candied orange-peel.

Oreille, F. Ear. *Oreille de porc,* F.—Pig's ear, etc.

Orge, F. Barley. *Orgeat*—barley water or almond milk; a favourite summer drink.

Origan, F. Wild marjoram, botanical name *origanum*.

Orloff. The name of a Russian family of high standing. Also the name of a magnificent diamond, owned by the Count Alexis Orloff. A number of dishes and garnitures are styled *à l'Orloff*.

Orly (à la), F. Also *Horly*. Name given to dishes prepared in a certain style. Usually slices of fish or meat coated with rich batter, and fried in deep fat.

Ortolan. A small bird, about the size of a lark, a native of the south of Europe. In Italy and the south of France they are fed on millet seed and other grains.

Os de Moëlle, F. Marrow-bone.

Oseille, F. Sorrel. A sour plant of green colour, used for soups, salads or as a vegetable.

Osso bucco, IT. A dish prepared from the middle part of a knuckle of veal cut in slices. These pieces are braised in a thin *demi-glace* with a brunoise of vegetables or *tomates concassées*.

Oublie, F. A thin pastry; a dessert biscuit.

Ours, F. Bear.

Outarde, F. Bustard.

Ovale, F. Oval; egg-shaped.

106

Ox-cheek. Mufle or palais de bœuf, F.

Oxo. A flavoured fluid beef juice combining beef extractives and beef fibrine. Handy for making bouillon, etc.

Ox-tail. Queue de bœuf, F. Used for soup, or as entrée.

Ox-tail Soup. Potage au queue de bœuf, F. Ox-tail soup is said to have been discovered as follows: During the Reign of Terror in Paris, in 1793, many of the nobility were reduced to starvation and beggery. The abattoirs sent their hides fresh to the tanneries without removing the tails, and in cleaning them the tails were thrown away. One of these noble beggars asked for a tail, which was willingly given him; he took it to his lodgings and made—what is now famous—the first dish of oxtail soup. He told others of his good luck, and they annoyed the tanners so much that a price was put on ox-tails.

Oxymel. Sour honey. Honey and vinegar.

Oyster. Huître, F. A bivalvular testaceous shellfish, highly esteemed on account of its delicious flavour and nutritive qualities. In season from September to April.

Oyster Plant. (*See* SALSIFY.)

Oyster Soup. This is prepared by cooking oysters slowly in their own liquor and white wine, cream is then added and crushed cracker biscuits used to thicken the preparation slightly.

Pabrica. (*See* PAPRIKA.)

Paillasse, F. A grill effected over hot cinders.

Paillé, F. Straw-coloured. *Paillettes*—straws (the word *Pailles* is more commonly used).

Pailles, F. Straws. As *Pailles au parmesan*—cheese straws. *Pommes de terre en pailles*—straw potatoes.

Pain, F. Bread. Also applied to small shapes of forcemeat; also fruit or cream purée. *Pain bis*—brown bread. *Pain* *fourré*—small rolls filled as sandwiches. *Pain mollet*—light bread. *Pain de ménage*—home-made bread. *Pain rôti*—toast. *Pain rassis*—stale bread. *Pain de seigle*—rye-bread. *Pain noir*—bread made of a mixture of wheat, rye, and buckwheat. *Pain d'épice*—a kind of gingerbread which has been in use ever since the 14th century. It was then made and sold only in Paris, according to Monteil (*Histoire des Français*). Gingerbread was introduced into England by the Court of Henry IV.

Pain de Volaille, F. Small moulds of finely-pounded chicken purée or farce.

Palais de Bœuf, F. Ox-palate.

Palma. Term applied to sherry, meaning "fine and dry."

Palomet. A species of mushroom.

Pamplemousse. Grape fruit. Shaddock.

Panaché, F. Mixed with two or more kinds of vegetables, fruits, etc.; also used for sweet creams.

Panada. Panade, F. A culinary paste of flour and water or soaked bread, used in the preparation of forcemeat, quenelles and for stuffing.

Panais, F. Parsnip. A plant of the carrot family, said to be of English origin.

Pancake. Crêpes or Pannequets, F. Thin flat cakes, made of batter and fried in an omelet pan. It is a peculiar fact that the French have adopted two English words in naming pancakes, "*crêpe*" is derived from the Old English word "*crisp*" or "*cresp*," under which name pancakes were known in Chaucer's time. "Pannequets" is derived from pancakes, as is easily noticed by the sound of the word.

Pané, F. Breaded, crumbed, dipped or rolled in breadcrumbs.

Panure, F. Breadcrumbs, grated crumbs, or bread raspings.

Panurette. A preparation of grated rusks, used for crumbing, for coating the inside of moulds, and for decoration in place of lobster coral.

Pâon, F. (*See* PEACOCK.)

Papaw. Papaye, F. A South American fruit, green in colour, and very similar to a small melon in appearance and flavour. It is eaten either raw or cooked. The sap of the tree and the juice of the fruit both possess the unique property of speedily rendering the toughest meat tender, and for this purpose meat and fowls are often hung among the branches of the tree to imbibe its exhalations.

Papier dentillé, F.   Lace paper.

Papillotes (en).   Paper capsules, cases or envelopes, greased, and fastened round cutlets, etc. Buttered paper answers the same purpose when twisted along the edges. The origin of paper bag cookery.

Paprika.   Hungarian red pepper. A kind of sweet capsicum of a brilliant scarlet colour, grown in Southern Europe; it is less pungent than the Spanish pepper. (*See* PIMIENTO.)

Parfait, F.   Perfect. A kind of light, rich ice-cream. A mixture of the soufflé type of fish, fowl or game, enriched with the essence of its chief ingredient.

Parfait-amour.   A French liqueur flavoured with grated citron peel.

Parisienne (à la), F.   Parisian Style. A surname applied to various kinds of dishes, principally meat dishes, which are dressed in a more or less elaborate style. No particular specification as to garnish or mode of cooking can be given, as these vary in almost every dish thus styled.

Parkin.   A variety of round, flat gingerbread, cakes or drop scones made of oatmeal, treacle, etc.

Parmentier (Antoine Augustin).   Born 1737, died 1813; introducer of the potato into France, in 1786, during the reign of Louis XVI. He also invented twenty different ways of cooking potatoes.

Parmesan.   Name of an Italian cheese, largely used for culinary purposes.

Parr.   (*See* SAUMONEAU.)

Parsley. Persil, F.   A native plant of Sardinia, introduced into England in 1548. Parsley is used for sauces and salads, and as a pot-herb. It makes a pretty garnish for dishes.

Parsnip. Panais, F.   The parsnip is considered a fattening vegetable. In times of scarcity, when wheat was dear and not easily procured, a very good bread was made from the roots of parsnips ground to flour.

Parson's Nose or **Pope's Nose.**   This name is given to the extreme end portion of the tail of a fowl. This, and the oyster of a fowl, constitute the French *sot-l'y-laisse*.

Partridge. Perdreau, or Perdrix, F.   Some variety of this bird is found nearly all over the world. The English bird has a finer flavour than the French partridge, the latter being known by the redness of its legs.

Passer, F. A word much used in cookery. To pass a sauce, soup, vegetable or meat, means to run it through a tammy cloth, sieve, or strainer. In the culinary language, the word "passer" has also the same meaning as "faire revenir," *i.e.,* to slightly fry in butter over a quick fire so as to form a crusty surface on meats or vegetables which are intended to be finished by some other process of cooking (usually stewing or braising).

Passoire, F. Colander; strainer.

Pastèque, F. A water-melon.

Pastillage, F. Gum paste, for ornamental confectionery, Pièce Montée, etc.

Pâte, F. Paste. *Pâte à frire*—frying batter. *Pâte d' Amandes*—almond paste. *Pâte d'Anchois*—anchovy paste. *Pâte croquante,* F.—Crisps almond and sugar paste. *Pâte feuilletée,* F.—Puff Paste. *Pâte frisée,* F.—Short crust paste. *Pâte pastillage*—gum paste.

Pâté, F. A pie; pasty; a savoury meat pasty, or a raised pie.

Pâté de Bifteck, F. Beefsteak pie.

Pâté de Foie-Gras, F. A well-known delicacy prepared from the livers of fat geese. Alsace is the most celebrated country where the so-called pâtés and terrines de foie gras are made. This delicacy was first introduced by a cook named Close.

Pâté de Périgord, F. Name of a French pie, which derives its name from Périgueux, a place celebrated for its truffles.

Patience. A vegetable similar to spinach. It has a specially mild flavour, with a slight acidity like sorrel leaves.

Pâtisser, F. To make pastry. *Pâtisserie*—pastry; a pastrycook's business. The word is also applied to a paste made of flour, salt, fat, and water, used to cover pies, etc. Also means all kinds of fancy tartlets. *Pâtissier*—pastrycook.

Patty. Pâté, F. A small pie or vol-au-vent of puff paste, filled with oysters or with game, fish, meat, etc., cut in dice, shreds, or pounded.

Paupiettes, F. Slices of meat rolled with forcemeat.

Pavot, F. (*See* POPPY.)

Paysanne (à la), F. Peasant's fashion. Prepared in a homely way.

Pea. Pois, F. The pea is, perhaps, the oldest known vegetable.

It existed in pre-historic times, peas having been found in the Swiss lake dwellings of the Bronze period. The three principal kinds of pea are the common field pea, the garden pea, and the sugar pea (*see* SUGAR PEA).

Peach. Pêche, F. There are two kinds of peaches, the cling-stone (or firm-fleshed) peaches, and the *fondant,* which are as soft and juicy as the mellowest apricot. Peaches grow in great abundance in the Channel Islands. The peach-tree was originally introduced by the Romans into Italy, from Persia, hence its name *persica,* which was ultimately corrupted to *Pêche.*

Peacock. Pâon, F. The peacock is a fowl of the pheasant kind, formerly a dish of much importance but now rarely eaten.

Pear. Poire, F. This fruit is divided into three classes, namely, dessert pears, pears for making perry, and stewing pears. The pear-tree was cultivated by the early Greeks and Romans.

Pêche, F. (*See* PEACH.)

Pectin. A substance which is contained in certain fruits, (quince, apples, plum, etc.) and vegetables (lentils, split peas, etc.) which, when boiled with sugar in the presence of enough acid causes thickening or jelling. Used in the manufacture of jam, jelly, flan glazes, etc.

Pemmican. Thoroughly-dried lean meat, powdered and mixed with melted fat or suet; currants and sugar are some-times added. An article of food largely employed by those hunting animals for their skins in North America.

Penguin. Pingouin, F. A genus of sea-fowls of Arctic regions. *Penguin eggs*—very large eggs imported from the western coast of the Cape Colony. These eggs are somewhat similar in texture and flavour to plovers' eggs.

Pepper. Poivre, F. Both white and black pepper are pro-cured from the seed of a small shrub which grows in various parts of India. The sole difference between the two is that in white pepper the outer husk of the seed is removed. As that can only be done with the best kinds, it forms an additional security that the pepper is good. Guinea Pepper—*poivre de Guinée.* Cayenne Pepper—*poivre de Cayenne,* or *poivre rouge.* These red peppers are prepared from the rye seeds of the chillie or capsicum pods, which are grown in Cayenne (Guiana), and Guinea, on the west coast of Africa, the latter being the more pungent variety. *Sauce Poivrade*—pepper sauce. *Poivré*—peppered.

Pepper Pot. A West Indian dish, consisting of stewed aromatic pork or bacon, shellfish, rice, vegetables, and pickled herbs, highly seasoned with cassareep and cayenne, and other peppers.

Perch. Perche, F. An excellent fresh-water fish. The flesh of this fish is as firm as that of the sole though not quite so rich. It is found in nearly all the British rivers and lakes.

Perdreau, F. Young partridge. *Perdrix*—full-grown partridge

Périgord or **Périgueuse (à la),** F. Perigord Style. This name is applied to dishes wherein a truffle sauce or a garniture consisting of truffles has been used.

Perles de Nizam and **Perles du Japon.** A special kind of large pearl barley.

Perry. Name of a beverage made of pears, corresponding to the cider made of apples. It contains little alcohol, and when preserved in casks or bottles it keeps good for some years.

Persil, F. (*See* PARSLEY.)

Persillade, F. A thick white sauce, in which a large quantity of parsley is used.

Pets-de-nonne, F. Ancient name for queen fritters or small *beignets soufflés.*

Petit Lait, F. Whey.

Petit Pain, F. Bread-roll. *Petits pains fourrés*—very small rolls scooped out and stuffed with various kinds of savoury purées; served as savoury or side dishes.

Petit Salé, F. Bacon. Lean salt pork.

Petite Marmite, F. A French soup. Beef and chicken broth.

Petits Fours, F. The generic name for all kinds of very small fancy cakes usually highly decorated with fancy icing, crystallised fruits, and bon-bons.

Petits Pois verts, F. Small green peas.

Petits Pois au Beurre, F. Green peas done in butter.

Petits Vols-au-Vent d'Huîtres, F. Oysters in pastry-cases.

Pétoncle, F. (*See* SCALLOP.)

Pettitoes. Pieds de porc, F. Pig's trotters.

Pheasant. Faisan, F. Generally regarded as the monarch of our game birds. The bird derives its name from the River Phasis, in Asia Minor, whence it was introduced into Europe.

112

Pheasant soup is becoming increasingly popular in this country; available in tins.

Philernum. Name of a West Indian liqueur, suitable for cups, punch, and flavouring, or as a liqueur.

Piccalilli. Mixed pickles, preserved in acidulated mustard sauce.

Picholine, F. A green olive, prepared to be eaten raw as a *hors d'œuvre.*

Pickle (to). To preserve fruit, vegetables, fish, or meat, in vinegar, brine, or in dissolved salt. *Mariner,* F.—To marinade or pickle.

Picnic. An outing into the country, combined with an *al fresco* meal.

Pie, Pâté, F. Meat, fish, or fruit baked in a dish covered with pastry. The most ancient form of pie is the pasty, which is made without a dish.

Pièce de Résistance, F. The principal joint or other important dish of a dinner. *Pièces montées*—centre-pieces; set pieces; mounted pieces.

Pied, F. Foot. *Pied d'âgneau, de porc, de mouton*—lambs', pigs', sheep's feet or trotters. *Pieds de Veau*—Calf's feet.

Pigeon, F. Pigeon. The many varieties of this bird are highly esteemed as an article of food. Bordeaux pigeon—*pigeon de Bordeaux.* Squab—*pigeonneau.* Wood pigeon—*mansard.* Rock pigeon—*biset.*

Pigeonneau au Cresson, F. Squabs with water-cress.

Pignolia. Pignon, F. Kernels of pine cones of warm countries; frequently used in place of almonds and pistachios.

Pig's Fry. The heart, liver, lights, and other interior parts of a pig.

Pike. Brochet, F. A fish known for its voracity, found in all the European lakes and rivers. Seasonable October to January.

Pilau, Pilaw, Pilaffe, F. A dish common in Egypt and Turkey, made of fish or poultry and rice. Also an Indian dish of meat or poultry and rice.

Pilchard. A fish resembling the herring, but much smaller.

Pilet, F. Pintail duck. A common migratory bird found in the north of England, Germany, and Holland.

Pimento. (*See* ALLSPICE.)

Pimiento. Red Spanish pepper-pod of sweet and pungent flavour; used for garnishing and in salads.

Pimpernelle, F.   Salad-Burnet. A herbaceous plant.

Pincer, F.   To pinch. To ornament or decorate paste before it is baked.

Pineapple. Ananas, F.   A much esteemed dessert fruit, native of South America, from whence it was first imported to Europe about the middle of the 18th century. Although the Hawaiian pineapples are considered the best, the large Kenyan variety which are also imported, are highly esteemed by many.

Pinson de Neige, F.   Snow bird.

Pintade, F.   Guinea-fowl. A bird of the turkey species of bluish-grey plumage, sprinkled with round white spots. *Pintadeau*—guinea chick.

Pintail. Canard pilet, F.   (*See* PILET.)

Piping.   To decorate or ornament with royal icing, creamed butter, etc., cakes, pastry, hams, galantines, etc.

Pippin.   A kind of apple. The Golden Pippin, Newtown Pippin, and Ribstone Pippin are all noted varieties.

Piquante, F.   Sharp of flavour, stimulating, pungent or sour.

Piquer, F.   To lard. *Piqué*—larded. To insert narrow strips of fat bacon, truffles, tongue, etc., into lean meat, poultry, game or fish.

Pissenlit, F.   (*See* DANDELION.)

Pistache, F.   Pistachio nut, used for flavouring and garnishing galantines, sweets, etc.

Pistache (en), F.   A term which describes a method of preparing a leg of mutton, partridges or pigeons in which the garnish consists of cloves of garlic.

Pitcaithly Bannock.   Name of a kind of Scotch shortbread, consisting of flat round cakes, the paste being made with flour, butter, sugar, almonds, peel, and caraway seeds.

Pithiviers.   A town of France, near Orleans, famous for its pastry, especially lark pies and almond tarts, and for its honey. The products are called *pithivériens*.

Plaice. Plie, F.   Flat sea-fish, seasonable May to November, belonging to the same order as the sole, flounder, and turbot. They are found in abundance on all the English coasts, but the best brought into our market are the Downs or Dover plaice, which are caught on the downs, or flats, between Hastings and Dover.

Planked steak.   Refers to a method whereby a thick steak, e.g.; an entrecôte is cooked on a well oiled, well seasoned

114

oak plank under a grill or salamander. It is then suitably garnished and taken to the table on the plank.

Plantain. Plantains closely resemble the banana in appearance and use. In some tropical countries they are baked in their skins, or sliced and fried in butter.

Plover. Pluvier, F. A bird whose eggs are esteemed a great delicacy. In season October to February. Plover eggs—*œufs de pluvier*. Plover's eggs are usually served as *hors d'œuvre*. *Pluvier doré*—golden plover.

Pluche, F. A garniture for soups. The leaves of parsley, chervil, tarragon, lettuce, and sorrel, cut into fine shreds. The name of a celebrated French writer of the 17th century.

Pluck. The heart, liver and lights of an animal.

Plum. (*See* PRUNE.)

Pocher, F. To poach. To parboil or to boil slightly. Mode of cooking usually applied to eggs and quenelles of fish, meat or game.

Poêle, F. A cooking pot or pan. *Poêler,* F.—To cook good quality meat or poultry in a covered pan, on a bed of root vegetables with butter. *Poêlon*—small skillet.

Point (à), F. Cooked to a turn.

Points d'Asperges, F. Tips or points of small green asparagus.

Poire, F. Pear.

Poireau, F. Leek (which see also). This vegetable is said to be a native of Switzerland. The leek was, and still is, the favourite ingredient for stocks, and especially in the soup known as "cock-a-leekie," of which King James I. was so fond that he retained his preference for it, notwithstanding all the dainties of French cookery. Leeks are also served as a vegetable course. The national emblem of Wales.

Pois, F. (*See* PEAS.). *Pois cassés*—split peas.

Poisson, F. Fish. The fish course of a dinner.

Poissonière, F. Fish-kettle; fish pan.

Poitrine, F. Breast.

Poivre, F. (*See* PEPPER.)

Poivre de Guinée, F. (*See* PEPPER.)

Polenta. A standard Italian dish made of Indian corn flour; in appearance and taste it is not unlike semolina.

Pollo con Arroz. A Spanish dish of chicken and rice.

Pollock. Colin, F. A sea-fish of the cod family.

Polonaise (à la), F. Polish Style. Various dishes are known under this name. Bortsch *à la Polonaise* and *Ragoût à la Polonaise* are types of dishes to which the peculiar flavour of cream, beetroot, and red cabbage is introduced.

Polony. A dry sausage made of meat partly cooked.

Polpetti. (*See* POULPETON.)

Pomegranate. Grenade, F. This fruit possesses great thirst-quenching properties in an exceedingly pleasant form. The fruit, when freshly gathered, is much larger than an orange. In its imported condition the pulp has diminished in quantity and deteriorated in quality, by the shrinking of the outer rind.

Pomme, F. (*See* APPLE.) *Beignets de pomme*—apple fritters. *Tarte aux pommes*—apple tart.

Pomme Cannelle, F. (*See* CUSTARD APPLE.)

Pomme d'Amour, F. (*See* TOMATO.)

Pomme d'Api, F. Small red and white French dessert apple. *Pommes sauvage*—crab-apple.

Pomme de Terre, F. Potato. Generally called *pommes* for short in Menus. *Pommes nouvelles*—new potatoes. *Pommes frites*—fried potatoes. *Pommes sautées*—tossed potatoes. *Pommes farcies*—stuffed potatoes. (*See* POTATO.)

Pompadour (Jeanne Antoinette, Marquise de). Born 1721, died 1764. Well known for her extravagance and indulgence in the luxuries of pleasure and eating. A number of dishes are styled *à la Pompadour.*

Pompelmoush. (*See* PAMPLEMOUSSE.)

Pont l'Evêque, F. A French cheese of delicate flavour.

Pope or **Ruffe.** A fish which very much resembles the perch in size, appearance, and flavour.

Pope's Eye. The name given to a small circle of fat found in the centre of a leg of mutton or pork. Also, in Scotland, the primest rump steak.

Pope's Nose. (*See* PARSON'S NOSE.)

Poppy Seed. Pavot, F. The capsule containing seed is the source whence opium is derived. It is said that there is only a small quantity of opium in the seeds themselves, which are used in stuffing mixtures and in cakes.

Pork. Porc, F. *Porc frais*—fresh pork. *Porc salé*—salted pork. *Peau de porc*—crackling.

Porridge. A Scotch dish. Oatmeal porridge is an everyday article of diet in Scotland. It is an agreeable as well as a nutritious article of food; served with cream or milk. Some people prefer to eat it with sugar, or butter, or even treacle.

Porringer. Name of a small dish in which porridge is served to children.

Port de Salut, F. A fine French cheese, of round flat shape.

Porterhouse Steak. A thick steak cut from the middle of the ribs of beef or sirloin.

Portugaise, F. Portuguese Style, usually some dish of which tomato forms a part.

Posset. Hot milk curdled with wine or acid; from the Welsh *Posel,* curdled milk.

Potage, F. Soup. *Potage Parmentier*—potato cream soup, so called because Parmentier introduced potatoes into France. *Potager*—soup-pot; cooking stove; kitchen garden.

Potato. Potatoes were first introduced into Europe in 1584 by Thomas Heriot, and were for a long time after considered a great delicacy, and could only be procured in small quantities at the price of 2s. per pound. After the middle of the 17th century they became gradually known and more extensively cultivated. In dietetic value the potato closely resembles rice.

Pot-au-feu, F. Is an economical and wholesome beef broth. It is the standard dish of all classes in France, and the origin of beef stock. The pot-au-feu no doubt originated in Spain, where it became the fashion to cook beef with vegetables; and from thence it was brought by Asmad, the chef of King Philip V., to France in 1715. (*See also* MARMITE.)

Pot-au-feu, Henry IV. A *pot-au-feu* is "a portion of beef destined to be treated in boiling water lightly salted so as to extract the soluble parts."—*Brillat-Savarin*. A king of France, Henry IV., promised that when he became king every peasant should be able to put a fowl in his pot every Sunday, and hence the *pot-au-feu* in which the *poule-au-pot* figures is styled Henry IV.

Potiron, F. Pumpkin or pompion. The fruit of an annual plant belonging to the gourd family. It grows in various shapes, the so-called pear-shaped species being most similar to the delicious marrow on English markets. It is used for the preparation of *potages,* such as *à la purée de citrouille*. It is also made in the form of a *choucroûte,* or *sauerkraut, au Potiron,* for winter use.

Potpourri, F.   A stew of various kinds of meats and spices; a favourite dish in Spain.

Potrock.   Name of a Russian thick soup.

Potted.   Fish or meat purée preserved in a pot,—*en terrine,* F.

Pottinger.   Ancient popular name for an apothecary or spice merchant.

Pouding, F.   Pudding. *Pouding au pain*—bread pudding. *Pouding au pain bis*—brown-bread pudding. *Pouding de Noel*—Christmas pudding; plum pudding.

Pougues.   A saline mineral water, the source of which is at Pougues, in the department of Nièvre, France.

Poularde, F.   Fat pullet; a chicken about 7 or 8 months old that has not started to lay eggs.

Poule, F.   The common hen. The expression is accepted as a culinary term, to imply a bird past the period at which it is tender enough to be roasted. It serves, however, well for invalid broth and for boiling under the name of *poule au riz. Poule au pot*—fowl boiled in the stock pot. *Poule d'eau*—water-hen, moor-hen. *Poule de neige*—white grouse.

Poulet, F.   Young cock chicken.

Poulet Dinde, F.   Young turkey.

Poulet de Grain.   Spring chicken. *Poulet à la Reine*—name given to fine specimens of young chickens. *Poulet en casserole*—chicken fried and basted with butter in an earthenware stewpan. When the chicken is browned in the butter the lid is put on the stewpan and it is allowed to cook slowly until done, being basted occasionally.

Poulette, F.   A hen chicken.

Poulette (à la), F.   A white sauce made of stock, butter, flour, egg-yolks, and chopped herbs. A white stew.

Poulpeton, F.   Slices of veal with minced meat.

Poultry.   Volaille, F.

Poupart, F.   A large crab, found on the coasts of France. Also called *tourteau.*

Poupelin, F.   A cheese cake.

Pourpier.   (*See* PURSLANE.)

Poussin, F.   A baby chicken, also known as chic-chicken or squab chicken.

Poutarge, Poutargue, properly **Boutargue,** F.   Botargo. A kind of dry caviare, pressed and prepared with the roe of haddock and of grey mullet (*mulet*). This somewhat strange dish, looking like a flat cake, is served in thin slices with oil and vinegar or lemon. A useful *hors d'œuvre*.

Praliné, F. Flavoured with burnt almonds. *Pralines*—a favourite sweet made with blanched sweet almonds, dipped in delicately-flavoured syrup which forms a rugged and delicious covering.

Prawn. Crevette rose, F. The common prawn is only a little larger then the shrimp, being from three to four inches in length, but prawns sent from Ireland are much larger. The best of them are known as Dublin Bay prawns.

Pré-salé, F. Mutton raised on the salt marshes of France. The word means "salt field," and the sheep to which it applies are mostly bred in the Ardennes and in the Brittany district called Dol. The flesh is darker than that of the ordinary animal, and moderately fat. The name is also applied to prime Southdown mutton.

Pressoir, F. An appliance for pressing grapes, apples, etc.

Présure, F. (*See* RENNET.)

Prickly Pear. Also called Indian fig. It is a pleasant wholesome, juicy fruit, imparting a peculiar cool sensation to the palate, and it is highly esteemed in the tropical countries where it grows.

Primeur, F. This usually implies edibles forced in order to be enjoyed out of their otherwise usual season. Strawberries, young carrots, turnips, tomatoes, beans, peas, and other vegetables obtained by hastening their growth, under glass or by any other means, are generally classed under that name.

Princesse, F. The name of a garnish in which asparagus tips are usually featured.

Printanier, F. Wherever this name is applied it always implies that a collection of early spring vegetables, left whole or cut small, is given, either as a garnish or in the form of macédoine. It is mostly used in connection with clear soups, removes, and certain ragoûts.

Printemps, F. Spring.

Processed Cheese. A product prepared from cheddar and other types of natural cheese, usually the hard pressed varieties. The natural cheese is broken down, finely ground and emulsified with certain salts (citrates and phosphates) and often water and whey powder. It is then heated and thoroughly mixed into a pliable homogeneous mass and packed in foil or other packaging material. It keeps well and need not be refrigerated. In N. America it is called process cheese.

Profiteroles, F.   These are made from choux paste piped on to a greased baking tin and baked. Various sizes are made depending on the intended use; very small for garnishes, hors d'œuvres, some sweet dishes etc. and for consommé; larger and filled with cream etc., for sweet dishes.

Protein.   An essential constituent of all animal and vegetable organisms. A good source of protein in the diet is milk because it contains all the essential amino acids required by the human body. A comparison with other foods illustrates this, *e.g.*; the protein in one pint of milk is approximately equivalent to that in 3 eggs or 1 lb. liver, beef steak or white fish.

Provençale (à la), F.   A description applied to certain French dishes, which generally implies that garlic or onion and olive oil have been used in their preparation.

Prune, F.   Plum. *Prune de reine-claude*—greengage plum. The English word prune is applied to dried plums.

Pruneau, F.   Dried plum.

Prunelle, F.   Sloe; wild plum.

Ptarmigan.   White grouse, or ptarmigan, are fond of high places, and are found even as far north as Greenland. Those seen in our markets come mostly from Norway and Scotland. They feed on the wild herbage of the hills, and this in a measure accounts for the slightly bitter, though not unpleasant, taste of the flesh. (*See* GROUSE.)

Ptomaines.   Name applied to certain poisonous substances found in decayed or tainted food which cause food-poisoning. Scientific authorities inform us the danger consists in germs, which have attacked or are bred in the food.

Puff Paste.   A rich paste used for covering pies and tarts and lining tartlets. Should be made with as little water as possible.

Puits d'Amour, F.   French pastry made of puff paste.

Pulled Bread.   Term applied to small pieces of bread; the crumb part of a loaf is pulled into pieces while hot, and baked in a moderate oven until they become crisp.

Pullet. Poulet, F.   A young hen or female fowl.

Pulque.   National beverage of Mexico, made from the juice of the maguey plant by means of fermentation, resembling butter-milk; not good after 48 hours.

Pumpernickel. Westphalian brown bread.

Pumpkin. Potiron, citrouille, F. This fruit is largely consumed by the Italian peasantry. It may be eaten raw, boiled as a vegetable, or made into soup or pies, and the young shoots may be dressed like spinach, which they resemble. The plant is supposed to be a native of the Levant. It grows in all warm climates, and in England it is cultivated in cucumber frames.

Punch. A species of hot or cold drink. "Punch" got its name from the Hindu word "panch," which means five. The Hindus made it with five ingredients—sugar, arrack, spice, lemon juice and water.

Punch à la Romaine, F., is a kind of soft white ice, made from lemon-juice, water, white of egg, sugar, and rum. It is served in goblets, usually after the remove; and it has the property of assisting considerably the functions of digestion. It forms a sort of interlude between two acts of that grand play—the dinner.

Purée, F. A smooth pulp; mashed vegetables; thick soups. The name is also given to meat or fish which is cooked, pounded in a mortar, and passed through a sieve. *Purée de pois*—pea soup.

Purée de Légumes, F. Vegetable purée.

Purée de Pommes de Terre. Potato purée; mashed potatoes.

Purslane. Pourpier, F. An American plant, used in salads, pot herbs, and pickles; first introduced into England in 1652.

Quadrillé, F. Checkered, thin strips of paste laid across tarts, so as to form a sort of net.

Quail. Caille, F. The quail is a small brown migratory bird of the partridge tribe. Enormous numbers arrive on the shores of the Mediterranean, from Africa, and are trapped and distributed thence throughout Europe, the flesh being delicate and much in demand at a time when game is out of season. In prime condition from September to January.

Quartier d'Agneau, F. A quarter of lamb. *Quartier de devant*—forequarter. *Quartier de derrière*—hindquarter.

Quass (quas, quaas). A Russian beer made of rye or bread, and also made of apples and pears. Widely used by the Russian white-collar classes.

Quassia Cup. An infusion of quassia chips, flavoured with orange peel, borage, and spices, sweetened and fortified with alcohol in some form.

Quenelles, F. Forcemeat of different kinds, composed of fish, poultry or meat, eggs, etc., shaped in various forms—balls, ovals, etc. They are used as garnishing for soups or entrées, or are served separately as entrées.

Queue, F. Tail. *Queue de bœuf*—ox-tail. *Queues d'écrevisse*—crayfish tails. *Queue de mouton*—sheep's tail. *Queue de veau*—calf's tail.

Quiche lorraine, F. A savoury flan with a filling made from eggs, lean bacon, cream or milk.

Quillet. A small alum cake. Dessert biscuits.

Quince. Coing, F. The quince is a yellowish-green, sour astringent fruit, of which some varieties resemble the apple, while others are more like the pear. Although their flavour is too harsh for eating raw, yet tarts, preserves, and marmalade may be made with them, and a little quince added to apple.

Quoorma. Name of a very mild Indian curry preparation.

Qutaif. Name of an Arabian dish similar to our pancakes; they are made as thin and leafy as possible, fried in almond oil, and are served up with a rich syrup, and besprinkled with rose water.

Rabbit. Lapin, F. (*q.v.*). A small rodent. Its flesh, though inferior to that of the hare, has a delicate flavour. Both wild and domesticated or tame rabbits are eaten. Ostend rabbits are bred for the market. Wild rabbit—*lapin sauvage,* F.

Rable, F. Back. Used only to designate the back or loin part or rabbit or hare. *Rablé* or *rablu*—thick backed.

Racahout, Racachou. An Arabian preparation consisting of the flour of roasted edible acorns, cocoa, potato flour, rice, sugar, salep (the powdered root of an orchid), and vanilla. It enjoys a certain reputation in France as a restorative nostrum. The name is also applied to a thin gruel given to invalids.

Racines, F. Root vegetables usually served as a garnish.

Rack. Arrack. (*See* ARAC.)

Radish. Radis, F. A salad plant with a pungent root. Some of the roots are long and tapering, other globular, the latter being commonly known as turnip radishes. Horse-radish — *Raifort.*

Raffinade. Best quality of refined sugar. *Raffiné* purified.

Rafraîchir, F. To refresh; to cool. *Glace à rafraîchir*—ice to put in drinks, etc.

Ragoût, F. A rich, seasoned stew of meat. The meaning of the word "ragoût" is to "give again taste," implying a combination of materials used together to impart taste to each other, which is brought about by the cooking process.

Rahat Lakoum. Turkish Delight.

Raie, F. Skate. A flat sea-fish. In season October to April.

Raifort, F. (*See* HORSERADISH.)

Raised Crust. A paste used for making meat and other savoury pies which do not require a dish. It is usually made with flour mixed into a stiff paste with boiling water and lard.

Raisin, F. Grape. The fruit of the vine, used as dessert, for jellies, ices, etc. *Raisin de Corinthe*—currant. *Raisin sec*—raisin.

Rakia. A Hungarian liqueur made from full-flavoured grapes.

Ramequin, F. Ramekin. Cheese fritter; a kind of cheese tartlet or ramekin. Savouries or small entrées served in ramekin or cases.

Ramereau, F. Young wild wood-pigeon.

Ramier, F. Wild wood-pigeon.

Ranhofer, Ch. A noted chef of Delmonico's Restaurant, New York, author of the "Epicurean," Franco-American cook book, a standard work in the United States. Died 1899.

Râper, F. To shred or grate.

Raspberry. Framboise, F. A fruit allied to the bramble; there are two kinds, the red and the white; both are used for compotes, tarts, and dessert. *Raspberry vinegar*—an acidulated syrup of raspberries.

Ratafia. The essence of bitter almonds, used for flavouring. There is also a liqueur flavoured with the kernels of plums, apricots, and peaches, to which the name is also given.

Raton, F. A kind of cheesecake.

Ratonnet, F. Small skewers of meat, generally of mutton.

Ravigote, F. A very richly-flavoured green herb sauce containing various herbs, vinegar, and garlic; served cold. First heard of in 1720. A French writer, Ducerceau, mentions it in one of his poems. There is also a hot sharp sauce with this name, prepared from a *Velouté* and herbs.

Ravioles or **Ravioli,** F. Very small squares or rounds of nouille paste enclosing a preparation of spinach, cheese, minced meat highly seasoned, etc. Served with a sauce and sprinkled with parmesan. Also used as soup garniture or as a savoury.

Réchaud, F. Warming dish. Chafing dish.

Réchauffé, F. Re-heated. Cold meat, etc., rewarmed or re-dressed.

Recherché, F. Exquisite; dainty.

Recrépi, F. Crimped. Applied to fish, salmon, cod or turbot.

Red Cabbage. Chou rouge, F. A species of the common cabbage with dark red leaves, chiefly used for pickling. In Germany, France, and Switzerland it is prepared as a vegetable, when it is shredded finely and stewed with rich broth.

Red Grouse. (*See* GROUSE.)

Red Herring. A cured and smoked fish principally eaten by the poorer classes. The flavour slightly resembles that of dried ham.

Red Mullet. Rouget or Rouget barbet, F. A highly esteemed fish, called the woodcock of the sea. This fish should not be gutted; the trail is supposed to be eaten when cooked. (Species *Mullus Barbatus*.)

Réduire, F. To boil down; to reduce; to boil liquid gradually to a desired consistency.

Réforme (à la), F. Named after the famous Reform Club of London. A garniture consisting of finely-cut strips of cooked carrots, truffle, ham, and hard-boiled white of egg. Also name of a brown sauce containing above items as garniture.

Refrigerator. A store chest or chamber containing ice, or a refrigerating plant, employed to maintain provisions at a low temperature.

Refroidi, F. Cooled; chilled.

Régal, F. Banquet; feast.

Régence, F. As a sauce applied to fish dishes it consists of a *Sauce Normande* with a reduction of white wine, garnished with sliced truffles and sliced mushrooms. A "sauce Régence" for meats consists of a "demi-glace" flavoured with truffles and white wine. For poultry and sweetbreads the sauce has a basis of "sauce allemande". Garnish "Régence" varies according to which of the above is applicable.

Réglisse, F. Liquorice.

Reims. A district in France famous for its champagnes.

Reindeer. Renne, F. A native of the Arctic regions, highly esteemed for its fine flavour. Reindeer tongues are a great delicacy.

Reine-Claude, F. Greengage. A variety of plum of superior richness and flavour to all other kinds of plums; name derived from Queen Claude, wife of François I. It was introduced into France over 400 years ago. Its English name is derived from the fact that Sir William Gage, of Hengrave Hall, near Bury St. Edmunds, obtained and cultivated cuttings from the French queen.

Reinette, F. Russet apple.

Relevé, F. The remove. A course of a dinner, consisting

of large joints of meat, four-footed game, and sometimes joints of fish. *Relever*—to remove; to turn up.

Relish. Goût piquante, F. A pleasing taste; to give an excellent flavour.

Remouillage, F. Second stock.

Rémoulade, F. A cold sauce, flavoured with savoury herbs and mustard, used as salad-dressing, etc.

Renaissance, F. A word applied to dishes, etc., introduced in the 16th century, and later.

Renne, F. (*See* REINDEER.)

Rennet. Présure, F., is the name given to the prepared inner membrane of a calf's, pig's, hare's, or fowl's stomach, which is used for curdling milk, The name is also applied to a liquid extract used in the manufacture of cheese.

Renversé, F. Turned out on a dish. Also applied to a caramel custard called *crème renversée*.

Repassé, F. Strained repeatedly.

Restaurant, F. A high-class eating-house. Originally the name of a soup invented by a Frenchman named Palissy in 1557. The soup consisted of finely-minced fowl, and broth highly spiced with cinnamon, coriander, etc. In 1765 a tavern was opened in Paris, under the title "Restaurant," for the purpose of supplying this wonderful soup.

Réveillon, F. Name given to a gastronomic festivity which takes place in France at Christmas Eve. It consists of a sumptuous supper, which is provided by the most wealthy and the most generous inhabitants of a town or village. This meal is served at midnight, when the *pièce de résistance* is usually *boudin noir,* black pudding.

Revenir (faire), F. To lightly fry or brown without actually cooking.

Rhubarb. Rhubarbe, F. A garden plant, the stalk of which possesses a peculiar acid flavour, and is used for puddings, tarts, etc.

Rhum, F. Rum. A spirit distilled from the fluid residuum of cane sugar, from molasses and saccharine by-products. Jamaica rum is considered the best, and is used for flavouring sweets, sauces, for omelets, hot drinks, etc.

Riblette, F. Collop of broiled or grilled pork.

Ribs of Beef. Côtes de bœuf, F. The wing rib *Côty d'aloyau,* F. —is considered the best. Fore rib—*côte première*.

Rice. Riz, F. An esculent grain of warm climates, largely used throughout Europe for puddings and soups. Although highly nutritious, it is not a perfect food, being deficient in albuminoids and mineral matters. It is supposed to be of Asiatic origin, but is now cultivated in the tropical regions of both hemispheres. There are many varieties of the plant, the chief being marsh rice, early rice, and mountain rice. Carolina rice is the best for puddings, and Patna for curries.

Richelieu (Armand Jean Duplessis, duc de). A celebrated gourmet, French general and cardinal during the reigns of Louis XIII. and XIV.; born 1585, died 1642.

Richelieu, Cardinal. Epicure, gourmet, churchman and politician, who is credited with having invented the sauce Mayonnaise, corrupted from Mahonnaise. His house, the Palais Cardinal, under its new name of Palais Royal, afterwards became a temple of *cuisine*.

Rillottes, F. A French potted meat preparation, used for *hors d'œuvre* and savouries. *Rillettes de Tours* are renowned.

Ris de Veau, F. Calf's sweetbread. *Ris d'âgneau*—lamb's sweetbread.

Ris de Veau piqué, F. Larded sweetbreads.

Ris Pisi. An Italian soup of rice and green peas.

Risotto. An Italian dish of rice, cheese, and usually tomato and saffron.

Rissolé, F. Well browned, fried, or baked; covered with crumbs.

Rissoles, F. Half-moon shapes of minced fish and meat mixtures, enclosed in paste, and fried. Also rolls of meat mixtures, egg and crumbed, then fried. *Rissolettes*—thin pancakes are used in place of paste.

Riz, F. (*See* RICE.)

Rizzared Haddie. (Scotch). Sun-dried haddocks.

Roach. Rouget grondin, F. A fresh-water fish, of the carp family. (Species *Leuciscus rutilus*.)

Roast (to). Rôtir, F. Roasting means cooking by radiant heat. This may be done by hanging meat from a jack or spit in front of a bright fire, or by rotating it on a spit in a rotisserie. The term is also applied to cooking meat in an oven.

Roasting Jack. This useful invention contains a spring which, when wound up, revolves a fly-wheel to which are attached hooks upon which the meat is hung.

Rob. (Arabic.) Inspissated fruit juice of the consistency of honey.

Robert, F. Name of a brown, spicy sauce, invented by a restaurant keeper of that name in Paris, 1789. Generally served with pork and similar meats which are difficult to digest.

Robe de Chambre (en), F. In dressing-gown. Paper cases filled with light iced cream. Potatoes cooked and served in their jackets.

Robine, F. A kind of pear, also known as *royale* and *muscat d'août*.

Rocambole, F. A kind of garlic, less pungent than the ordinary. Spanish shallot.

Rocket. Roquette, F. A salad plant, genus crucifera.

Roe (fish). Laitance, F.

Rognon, F. Kidney. *Rognons de veau*—calf's kidneys. *Rognons de mouton*—sheep's kidneys.

Rognon de Coq, F. Cock's kernel.

Rognures, F. Remnants; parings; trimmings.

Rollmops. Rolled, pickled herring fillets.

Romaine, F. Cos lettuce.

Romaine (à la), F. Roman Style.

Romanoff. The family name of the Russian Imperial family.

Romarin, F. Rosemary, a herb from a fragrant and pungent plant.

Rompre, F. To break. To work paste or dough two or three times.

Rook. The flesh of this bird is rather dry and somewhat coarse in flavour. Rooks should be stewed, or baked in a pie, never roasted.

Roquefort, F. A highly-esteemed French cheese, made with sheep's milk.

Roquette, F. (*See* ROCKET.)

Rosette, F. A term used to describe small round pieces of meat cut from a boned loin or best end of lamb. (*See also* NOISETTE.)

Rosolio. Rossolis, F. An Italian liqueur, flavoured with rose leaves, orange flowers, cinnamon, etc.

Rossini. Name of a famous musician. *Filet à la Rossini* was his own invention. Nowadays applied to tournedos, sautéed in butter, garnished with a slice of foie gras and truffle and masked with a madeira sauce.

Rôti, F. The roast, indicating the course of a meal which is served before the entremets. Roast meat, poultry, and game. *Rôti, rôtie*—roasted. *Rôtissoire*—roasting pan.

Rouge de Rivière. A kind of wild duck.

Rouget, F. Red mullet, a highly-esteemed fish called the woodcock of the sea.

Rouget or **Rouget Barbet,** F. (*See* RED MULLET.) The name *Rouget* is also loosely applied to various fresh-water fishes with reddish scales, among them the *grondin* (*q.v.*)

Roulade, F. Meat roll, rolled meat, small galantines. *Roulardines*—small rolls. *Roulé*—rolled.

Rousselet, F. Russet pear.

Roux, F. A preparation of butter and flour, used for thickening soups and sauces. There are three kinds of *roux,* white, fawn, and brown.

Royal. Royale, F. Name of an egg custard used for garnishing clear soups. Also the name applied to an icing (glace royale) made with whites of egg and icing-sugar, and used for coating and decorative purposes.

Royan, F. A delicately-flavoured small fish similar to sardines.

Ruban, F. Ribbon. *Rubané*—ribbon-like. Decorated with ribbons.

Rum. A spirituous liquor distilled from molasses, saccharine by-products, or the fluid residuum of the cane sugar manufacture.

Rumford. An American statesman and inventor of economical soups.

Rusks. Twice baked slices of cake or milk bread, sweet or plain. In making them the dough is baked in a square tin, and when cold cut into slices and rebaked in a slow oven.

Russe (à la), F. Russian style. Many dishes with this name are characterized by the use of sour cream, *e.g.*; *Bortsch à la russe.* The term may also mean that caviar is included.

Rutabaga. A Swedish turnip.

Rye. Seigle, F. In appearance this grain is similar to barley. It is indigenous to Southern Russia, but is now generally cultivated throughout N. Europe and N. America. In Russia a drink called "quass" is made from it, and the Americans distil whisky from it. Its nutritive value, measured by the amount of gluten it contains, stands next to wheat.

129

Rye Bread. Pain de Seigle, F. Rye flour is made into bread and cakes similar to the Scotch oatmeal cakes.

Sabayon, F. A light frothy sweet sauce composed of sherry or other white wine, cream or milk, sugar and eggs. (*See* ZABYAJONE.)

Sable, F. A kind of short-cake pastry. *Gâteau sablé*—sand cake.

Sabot au Sang, F. A stew prepared in olden times.

Saccharine. Saccharine has 300 times more sweetening power than sugar (diabetic and obesity). It has no impure qualities in common with sugar; the latter is an article of food, supplying nutrition to the human body; saccharine has no such quality. Its value as a sweetener stops with the palate.

Saccharometer. *Pèse sirop,* F. An instrument used to test the degree of sweetness of syrups, etc.

Sack. A wine used during the middle ages; originally produced in the Canary Islands. *Sack posset*—a drink made of sack, milk, etc.

Saddle of Mutton. Selle de mouton, F. Consists of two loins undivided. Saddle of lamb—*selle d'agneau,"* F.

Saffron. Safran, F. A plant belonging to the crocus species; native of Asia Minor, but largely cultivated in the south of Europe. It is used for colouring and flavouring in culinary operations. *Saffron* from very early ages had a great medicinal reputation. Now, however, it is chiefly used as a harmless colouring ingredient for other medicines, in confectionery, and culinary preparations. It is the dried stigmas of the common crocus which grows so abundantly in our gardens. From 1582 till 1768 it was largely cultivated for yielding saffron in Essex at the place now called in consequence, Saffron Walden, and in Cambridgeshire. The saffron crocus has large purple or violet flowers, and blooms in the autumn, not in spring. The stigmas are gathered by women and children and are spread out on a cloth to dry in the sun. One grain of saffron contains the stigmas of nine flowers— *i.e.,* 4320 go to the ounce. Saffron is of a rich orange colour, has a bitter taste and an aromatic odour.

Sage. Sauge, F.   A European herb used as a flavouring for goose-stuffing, etc.

Sago. Sagou, F.   The farina from the sago palm-tree, a native of tropical countries, particularly Molucca. Sago is obtained from the trunk of this tree when slit open.

Saignant, F.   Underdone. Generally applied to steaks and game.

Saindoux, F.   Hog's lard. Used for frying; also for modelling purposes, socles, flowers, etc.

Saisir (faire), F.   To seize; to cook meat over a brisk fire to make it retain its juices.

Saki.   A Japanese liquor, distilled from rice.

Salad Dressing.   A combination of yolk of egg, mustard, salt, pepper, olive oil, cream and vinegar.

Salade, F.   Salad. Raw herbs, edible plants, raw and cooked vegetables, etc., seasoned with oil and vinegar or other salad dressing. *Saladier*—salad dish or bowl.

Salade de Légumes, F.   Vegetable salad.

Salamandre, F.   Formerly a utensil which after being made red hot was used for browning the surface of dishes requiring colour. Nowadays the term is used to describe electric and gas appliances which fulfil this function.

Salami.   An Italian sausage, chiefly used as *hors d'œuvre,* and for sandwiches.

Salé, F.   Salt, salted; corned. *Saler,* F.—To salt; to season with salt. *Saler de le viande*—to cure meat. *Salière*—salt cellar.

Saleratus. (American).   Bi-carbonate of soda. Bread made with this, and salt. Soda bread. Said to be responsible for much of the dyspepsia common in the States.

Salicoque, F.   (*See* PRAWN.)

Sally Lunn.   Name of a kind of tea-cake, slightly sweetened and raised with brewers' yeast. Sally Lunn was a celebrated personage at Bath who, at the close of the 18th century, used to make and sell a kind of tea-biscuits known as Sally Lunns. She used to sell these in the streets of Bath.

Salmagundi. Name of a very old English supper dish. It is a kind of meat-salad, mixed and decorated with hard-boiled eggs, anchovy, pickles, and beetroot.

Salmi or **Salmis,** F. A brown ragoût made of game when par-roasted. The term is also incorrectly applied to a réchauffé of previously cooked game.

Salmon. Saumon, F. The salmon, which leaves the sea and ascends the river to spawn, is one of the most delicious and nutritive of the finny tribe, although less easily digested than fish containing less fatty matter. Salmon are found distributed over the north of Europe and Asia, but not in warm latitudes, never having been caught so far south as the Mediterranean. The salmon is said to grow quickly. Izaak Walton says: "The samlet becomes a salmon in as short time as a gosling becomes a goose." (*See also* GRILSE.)

Salmon trout, truite saumonée, F. Although salmon trout resemble salmon in appearance and flavour they are in fact of a different species. This trout has pink flesh when small and is generally used when up to 2–3 lbs. in weight. Recipes for salmon and trout are applicable to salmon trout.

Salpêtre, F. Saltpetre. The commercial name for nitre, the nitrate of potash; used in conjunction with salt, etc., for curing meat.

Salpicon, F. A mince of poultry or game with ham or tongue and mushrooms used for croquettes, bouchées, rissoles, etc.

Salsify. Salsifis, F. Oyster plant. The flavour of the root which is white resembles somewhat that of the oyster. (*See* SCORZONERA.)

Salt. Sel. F. Salt in a mineral form is salt in its native form, as it is found deposited in the earth. Sea or crude salt or gray salt is the product of the evaporation of sea water by the action of the sun, wind or frost, or of the water of salt lakes. Washed salt is obtained by bleaching sea salt. Refined salt or white salt, so called table salt, is obtained by the crystallisation of saturated solutions of rock or sea salt, either naturally or artificially.

Salt Fish. Morue sèche, F. Cod, ling and other large fish are frequently salted when newly caught and either kept in pickle or dried by air. The dried kind requires soaking in cold water for from 24 to 36 hours before being cooked, while that taken out of the pickle-tub also requires soaking for several hours before cooking.

Salzgurken, G. Small salted cucumbers. German pickle served with boiled or roast meats; made of cucumbers soused in salt water.

Samp. A food composed of coarsely-ground maize, boiled, and eaten with milk (American dish).

Samphire. A herb used for salads and pickles. Grows by the sea-shore, generally on the cliffs.

Samztah. An Arab dish, consisting of sweet purée or cream, dates, and cornflour.

Sand Grouse (*Pterocles arenarius*) is not related to the true grouse, which belongs to the game bird family. *Pterocles* has affinities with pigeons and plovers. It ranges from the Canaries, North Africa and Madagascar, to South Europe and Central Asia; everywhere it is a bird of the desert.

Sanders. May be described as miniature "Shepherd's Pies." Minced beef or mutton with a little onion, gravy, and seasoning is put into saucers or scallop shells, covered with mashed potato, and browned in the oven.

Sandre, F. Pike, perch; wall-eyed perch.

Sandwich. Tartine, F. Originally two thin pieces of bread, buttered, with a thin slice of meat or meat paste between them, now the filling may be savoury or sweet. The name is supposed to be derived from the Earl of Sandwich. *Bookmaker sandwich,* two long slices of bread cut from a half quarton with a grilled entrecôte steak in between. *Club sandwich*—A sandwich in layers, made from toasted bread, slices of chicken, lettuce, mayonnaise and grilled bacon.

Sangaree. The name of an Indian punch drink. It is made with sherry, water, lemon-juice, and sugar.

Sangler, F. To prepare the ice mixture ready for freezing. One part of salt to five parts of broken ice is the proper proportion used for freezing.

Sanglier, F. Wild boar.

Santos. A city and seaport of Brazil. Brazilian coffee—product of the state of São Paulo.

Sapaceau, F. An egg punch.

Sapote, F. Sapota. A West Indian fruit.

Sarbotière, F. (*See* SORBETIERE.)

Sarcelle, F. Teal. Water-fowl similar to wild duck. Seasonable October to February. Sometimes wrongly applied to widgeon (*macreuse*), and other fowl of the wild duck tribe.

Sardine, F. A little fish, generally preserved in oil and packed in hermetically-sealed tins or glass pots; served as a *hors d'œuvre,* etc. Those caught on the French coast are considered to be the best. This little fish is said to derive its name from having been first preserved in Sardinia. Some of the cheaper kinds are merely sprats or pilchard.

Sardines grillées, F. Broiled or grilled sardines.

Sarrasin, F. Buckwheat.

Sarsenage, F. A cheese similar to Roquefort.

Sasarie. A South African dish, similar to hâtelettes, but the meat is laid in a curry mixture for 3 days before being cooked.

Sassafras. The name of an agreeable beverage much drunk in North America.

Sasser, F. To stir—to take up a spoonful from the bottom of a pan and drop it back.

Sauce, F. Sauce. A liquid seasoning served and eaten with food, to improve its relish and to give flavour. The four great sauces in the culinary art are: Espagnole, Béchamel, Velouté, and Allemande. *Saucer,* F.—To sauce a dish; to cover with a sauce. *Saucier,* F.—Sauce cook. *Saucière,* F.—A sauce-boat; a deep, narrow-shaped dish or bowl, in which sauce is served.

Saucisse, F. Sausage. Fresh pork sausages. *Saucisson,* F.— Smoked sausages. (*See* SAUSAGE.)

Sauerkraut, G. Choucroute, F. A kind of pickled cabbage; finely-shredded cabbage preserved in brine. A national dish of Germany. Served hot with bacon or sausages.

Saugrené, F. A French process of cooking, implying stewed with a little water, butter, salt, and herbs, *e.g., pois à la saugrenée* are stewed peas cooked as above described.

Saumon, F. (*See* SALMON.) Jowl—*tête*. Tail—*queue. Petit saumon*—salmon grilse.

Saumoneau, F. Samlet; a very small young salmon, or parr.

Saumure, F. A culinary bath, brine, or pickle.

Saumuré, F. Pickled, or marinaded.

Saupiquet, F. Spiced vinegar sauce.

Sauré, F. Fried or cured in smoke.

Saurin. A red herring; a freshly-cured herring.

Sausage. Saucisse, F. Wurst, G. Claimed to have been invented by a German in 1805.

Sauté-pan. Sautoire, F. A shallow, thin-bottomed cooking pan.

Sauter, F. A culinary term, indicating a quick cooking process. To toss over heat, in a sauté or frying-pan with little butter or fat anything that requires a sharp heat and quick cooking.

Sauterne. A French white wine (white claret) much used in cookery.

Savarin (Brillat-). Born 1755. Famous gastronomic writer; author of the excellent work entitled "Physiologie du Goût, ou Méditations de Gastronomie Transcendante," published after his death. A light spongy yeast cake is named after him.

Saveloy. A kind of smoked pork sausage; it is highly seasoned, and has an addition of saltpetre to give the meat a red colour.

Savory. An aromatic herb of the same class as mint. Two kinds are cultivated in England, one of which is fit for use in winter and the other in summer; they are, therefore, called respectively "winter" and "summer" savory.

Savoury. Savoureux, F. Tasty, well-seasoned tit-bit; denotes the final course of a complete dinner.

Savoy. The savoy is a hardy variety of the cabbage improved by frost, and in season throughout the winter. Also name of a kind of sponge cake.

Scald. To scald milk is to bring it nearly to the boil.

Scallop or **Escallop.** Pétoncle, F. A shellfish. This mollusc is similar in appearance to an oyster, only much larger. Seasonable from September to March, and at its best during January and February. Only the muscular part or heart is eaten. It is white, and when at its best the ova—or tongue, as it is commonly called—is full, and of bright orange colour. Scallops are prepared in numerous ways for the table; as stews in white sauce, scalloped, *au gratin* or *sauté,* as fritters, and sometimes in salads.

Scampi, IT. See Dublin Bay Prawns.

Scarlet Runner. A string bean resembling the French beans, the pods of which are eaten in the same way. They come, however, a little later in the season, and are a little coarser in flavour.

Schalet, Cholet. A Jewish Sabbath dish of meat, rice, and peas (or barley and peas), set on the fire on Friday and allowed to cook until Saturday.

Schenkeli. A kind of pastry; small rolls fried in butter; very popular in Switzerland.

Schiedam, Schnapps. A Holland gin liqueur distilled from grain and flavoured with juniper berries.

Schlesisches Himmelreich, G. A Silesian speciality consisting of sauerkraut and purée of peas.

Schmorbraten. A German dish, consisting of rump of beef braised (*à-la-mode* fashion), garnished with mushrooms, gherkins, and braised vegetables.

Schnitzel. A term much used in Germany and Austria. A thin slice of meat, chiefly veal.

Schwarzbrod. German rye, or brown bread.

Scone. A variety of tea cake, originally cooked on a griddle or hot-plate. (Scotch origin.)

Score (to). To make incisions crossways on the surface of fish, vegetables or meat. This is done to facilitate the process of cooking, and thus improving the flavour.

Scorsonère, F. Scorzonera. The same as salsify (*q.v.*), but the root is black.

Scotch Eggs. Name given to a dish of hard-boiled eggs; the shells having been removed, they are covered with a layer of sausage or other forcemeat, after which they are egged and crumbed and fried in deep fat.

Scotch Kail. Name of a thick broth; a kind of pot-au-feu, served as a standing dish among the middle classes of Scotland, of which kale or kail is a component part.

Scottish Style. à l'Ecossaise, F.

Scotch Woodcock. Toast spread with anchovy paste, with scrambled eggs on top.

Sea Bream. Brême or dorade der mer, F. A fish plentiful on the shores of Cornwall, and on the southern coast, especially near Hastings. When young, this fish is known as the Chad.

Sea Cucumber. (*See* TREPANG.)

Sea Kale. Chou der mer, F. A delicious vegetable largely cultivated in Great Britain, but very little known on the Continent; it grows wild in all parts of Europe. It was first grown in England in the middle of the 18th century by a gardener in Stoke Fleming, who cultivated the plants, which he found growing wild. They were so much appreciated that the gardener's master presented some of the roots to his friends at Bath, after which they became popular in all parts of England.

Sea Slug. (*See* TREPANG.)

Seasoning, E. Assaisonnement, F. That which is used to render food palatable and more relishing. The word is also employed to include forcemeat and stuffing.

Sec, Sèche, F. Dry. Of champagne (using masculine, *sec*), meaning that a little liqueur has been added to make it less sweet. *Séché,* F.—Dried. *Sécheur,* F.—A drying apparatus.

Sect. A German disignation for champagne. From the Latin, *vino secco,* dry wine.

Seigle, F. (*See* RYE.) *Pain de seigle,* F. Rye bread. Rye bread is very nutritious, and keeps fresh for a longer period than wheaten bread.

Sel, F. Salt (chloride of sodium). Used for seasoning food, for preserving and freezing purposes. (*See also* SALT.)

Selle, F. Saddle. *Selle de mouton,* F.—Saddle of mutton.

Seltz (Eau de Seltz), F. Selters or Selterwasser, G. A well-known mineral water.

Semolina. Semoule, F. Made from decorticated wheat by grinding pressure and heat. In this country it is chiefly used for puddings and thickening soups, but in France it is much esteemed for making the fine, white bread called "gruau."

Serviette, F. Table napkin. *En Serviette*—served in a napkin, or dished up in a napkin.

Sévigné, F. *A French soup named after the Marchioness* Sévigné of Rabutin-Chantal, a French authoress, born 1626, died 1696.

Shad. A salt-water fish fond of ascending rivers. Within comparatively recent years was caught near Hampton Court.

Shaddock. A large and coarse species of orange, named from Captain Shaddock, who first introduced it into the West Indies from China in the 17th century. Called pomeloe in the East. (*See* PAMPLEMOUSSE.)

Shallot. (*See* ECHALOTE.)

Shandy Gaff. A mixture of ale and ginger beer.

Shank Jelly. A kind of savoury jelly, lightly seasoned, recommended to weak people.

Sharks' Fins. Considered great delicacies by the Chinese, who pay high prices for this dainty. But shark's flesh as a rule is strong and rank, though firm, boneless, and nourishing.

It is said that fish of the shark family, and especially the dog-fish, are largely used by London fried-fish shop keepers.

Sharp Cheese. One that is well matured with a strong sharp flavour.

Sherbet. A cooling drink consisting of water, tartaric acid, lemon-juice, and sugar. The word Sorbet is derived from Sherbet.

Sherry Cobbler. An American drink, made with soda-water, sherry, and sugar, a dash of liqueur, and a little rice.

Shin of Beef. Jarret de bœuf, F. The fore portion of a leg of beef. Used for stock, for making soups, etc.

Shot Pepper. This is mignonette pepper, which is made from white peppercorns. It is broken into grains or granulated about the size of mignonette seed.

Shred. Is to slice anything so finely with a sharp knife that the shreds curl.

Shrimp. Crevette, F. A small sea crustacean.

Shrub. A drink. Orange-juice, zest, and rum punch.

Sikbaj. Name of an Arab stew made of sheep's head.

Sillsillat. A Swedish dish; a kind of herring salad.

Silverside of Beef. This joint is cut from the top of the round of beef. It is very good boiled, either salted or fresh.

Simnel Cake. A Lenton or Easter cake, with a raised almond crust, coloured with saffron, the interior being filled with the materials of a very rich plum-pudding. They are made up very stiff, boiled in a cloth for several hours, then brushed over with egg, and baked.

Singe (to). To pass a plucked bird over a flame so as to burn off the down which may have been left on. A spirit lamp is best for this purpose.

Singer, F. To dust with flour from the dredging-box.

Sippets. Small slices of bread cut into different forms fried or toasted, served as garnishing with meat entrées, or for borders of savoury dishes.

Sirloin. Aloyau, F. The sirloin of beef is said to owe its name to King Charles II., who, dining off a loin of beef, and being well pleased with it, asked the name of the joint. On being told, he said, "For its merit, then, I will knight it, and henceforth it shall be called Sir Loin." In an old ballad this circumstance is thus mentioned:

> "Our Second Charles, of fame facete,
>   On loin of beef did dine;
> He held his sword, pleased, o'er the meat,—
>   'Arise, thou famed Sir Loin!'"

It is also said however, that the derivation is from the French *surlonge*.

Sirop, F. Syrup. *Siroper,* F.—To mask with or steep in syrup.

Skate. (*See* RAIE.)

Skewers for Joints, etc. Brochettes, Hâtelets, etc., F.

Skim Milk. Name given to that part of milk left after the cream has been separated.

Skink. (Scotch). A strong beef soup.

Slapjack or **Flapjack.** Tôt-fait, F. A kind of pancake.

Sling. A drink made of rum and water, sweetened. Also applies to other drinks, e.g., gin with ice, sugar, sliced orange or lemon, and a little mint or borage.

Sloe. Prunelle, F. The fruit of the blackthorn.

Smelt. Eperlan, F. A most delicious little fish, its principal characteristic being the cucumber smell which is most pronounced. The only legitimate way of cooking this fish is frying in deep fat. Usually served with lemon and thinly cut slices of brown bread and butter.

Smoked. Fumé, F.

Smörgasbord (Smögerspud). Swedish name for hors d'œuvre.

Smörrebröd. Danish name for appetizers, particularly open type sandwiches.

Snail (Edible). (*See* ESCARGOT.)

Snipe. Bécasse, F. A small marsh bird whose flesh has a delicate flavour. Snipe are not natives of Britain. They mostly come over at the beginning of winter, and take their flignt again in the spring, then passing towards Lapland, Poland, Russia, Iceland, and Sweden.

Snoek. A South African fish. Imported in hermetically-sealed tins.

Snow. Neige, F. Name given to a froth of cream whipped up, or whisked white of egg and sugar, to which any desired flavour may be added which does not alter its white colour. Snow is often used as a covering of sweet dishes and for decorative purposes.

Socle, F. Base. Pedestal or ornamental stand. Made of rice, fat, sugar, etc., formerly much used in cookery and confectionery.

Soissons. Haricots blancs, F.   French white beans.

Soja.   The fermented juice of the soya bean. (*See also* SOY.)

Sole.   A marine flatfish of most excellent flavour. Its flesh is white, delicate, and nutritive. It abounds on the British coasts, Torbay yielding the finest specimens. Its colour, as well as its flavour, depends in a great measure on its food, which consists mostly of small crabs and other shell-fish, and the characteristics of the ocean bed where it is found. If very light in colour, it is called the white sole; if muddy, the black sole, the latter being considered the best. Lemon sole—*limande,* F. Slips—*petite sole,* F.

Solferino.   An Italian village, the scene of two great battles. A clear soup, with small batter quenelles, tomato and other vegetable garnish, is so named. Also describes a blend of tomato and potato soup.

Sommélier, F.   Wine steward or waiter.

Sorbet, F.   An iced Turkish drink; also the name of a soft water ice with fruit or liqueur flavour, usually served in goblets.

Sorbetière, F.   A pewter freezing-pot or freezing-pan.

Sorrel. Oseille, F.   A plant more or less acidulous from the presence of oxalic acid and potash.

Sot-l'y-laisse, F.   Rump or oyster of the chicken. Literally translated, "The fool leaves it." (*See* PARSON'S NOSE.)

Soubise, F.   Name given to a smooth onion pulp served with various kinds of meat entrées. The name is supposed to come from Prince Charles Soubise (born 1715, died 1787), who was a celebrated epicure. He served as field-marshal during the reign of Louis XIV. of France. As a surname to dishes à la soubise is generally applied when onions enter largely into the composition of a dish; the term usually implies a strong onion flavour, or a garnish of onion purée.

Souchets or **Souchies.**   Probably derived from the word "souche," stump or piece. Often used with the prefix "water-," as water-souchet (*q.v.*). It consists of a flat fish, as flounders or soles, cut transversely in slices, boiled in salted water, and served with finely-shredded roots and herbs.

Soufflé, F.   A very light baked or steamed pudding; an omelet. Also applied to light savoury creams. *Soufflé glacé,* F.-

—A very light sweet cream mixture, iced, and served in *soufflé* cases.

Soult. A South African dish. Pig's trotters boiled till tender and then marinaded for some days—eaten cold.

Soupe, Potage, F. Soup. Spring soup. Potage printanière, F. *Soupière*—soup-tureen.

Soupe à l'Oignon, F. Onion soup.

Souper, F. Supper; evening meal. *Souper de bal,* F.—Ball supper.

Souper sur l'Herbe. A kind of picnic supper, each guest bringing his basket of provisions with him. Supper is partaken on the floor, which has previously been strewn with grass. The room is decorated with shrubs and hot-house plants to imitate a field or garden.

Sour. Aigre, F.

Souse. A liquid in which meat or fish is soaked.

Southern fried chicken. Chicken cut in joints floured, fried and then finished in the oven.

Soy. Soja. Soya, F. This is a preparation added to soups and sauces as a flavouring and colouring ingredient. It is said to be produced by fermentation of the soja-bean in salt water. It is shipped to this country as a dark brown treacle-like extract. Cautiously mixed with certain soups, ragoûts, sauces, and gravies, it imparts, an agreeable flavour and improves the colour.

Soyer, Alex., 1809–59. A notable French chef who advocated English dishes prepared in French Style. Great culinary reformer. Went to Ireland 1848 to cook during the famine, and to Crimea 1854. Was chef at the Reform Club, invented a camp stove, wrote "The Poor Man's Cookery Book" and "A Culinary Campaign."

Spaghetti. A kind of very small macaroni.

Spare Rib of Pork. The back of a pig's neck is peculiarly well-covered with flesh, especially that of a large animal destined for bacon. This portion, including the ribs attached, is called the "spare rib." In some localities in the North, the backbone (chine), and the ribs with their lean flesh, is separated from the side or flitch, and eaten in a fresh condition. The term spare-rib is also applied to this.

Sparrowgrass. Vulgar name for asparagus.

Spatchcock. Originally a fowl, killed and immediately roasted or broiled, for some sudden occasion. The name is said to be a corruption of despatch and cock. The modern dish consists of a chicken split down the back, flattened out, and grilled. (*See* SPREAD EAGLE.)

Spatule, F. Spatula; a flat wooden spoon or knife used for spreading icing and other soft usbstances.

Spice. Épice, F. Condiment used for highly-seasoned food.

Spinach. Epinard, F. A favourite green vegetable. As a culinary remedy considered to have a direct effect upon complaints of the kidneys. Spinach is said to have originally come for Persia, and was undoubtedly employed for medicinal purposes by the ancient Arabian physicians.

Spongada. Italian preparation of semi-frozen water-ice and stiffly-whipped white of eggs.

Sprat. Melette, F. A small, cheap, but useful fish, allied to the herring. They are eaten whole, usually boiled or grilled.

Spread Eagle Chicken. Poulet à la Crapaudine, F. A young fat chicken split down the back, flattened, breast-bone removed, seasoned, oiled or buttered, and grilled or baked.

Spring of Pork. The thin flank or breast and belly.

Spruce Beer. Beer to which is added, during fermentation, an extract of the tops of the spruce fir.

Squab. A young pigeon; name used particularly in North America. *Squab chicken*—a young chicken. Applicable to animals while young, fat, and clumsy. Squab pie is therefore primarily a (young) pigeon pie. Such a pie becomes Devonshire squab pie by the addition of apples. *Squab-pigeons*—innocents.

Squash. (*See* VEGETABLE MARROW.)

Squid or **Calamary** or **Cuttlefish.** (Sêche, F.) The body can be cut into slices, (skinned by blanching) breadcrumbed or passed through batter and deep fried. Squid is available frozen or dried form or in cans. In parts of France they are stuffed and braised slowly.

Stachys. (*See* CHINESE ARITCHOKE.)

Starch. Amidon, F. Is found in some of the parts of nearly all plants, and abundantly in the forms of oats, barley, wheat, arrowroot, and potatoes. By the action of dilute acids and ferments, starch yields a number of sugar-like bodies known as glucose, dextrose, etc. Starch is not soluble in cold water, but when heated with water it swells considerably.

Starter. A term used in American and increasingly in England for first courses, appetisers, *hors d'œuvres,* etc.

Steak. A slice of meat, generally beef, which is to be grilled, roasted or fried. Its Danish equivalent is *Steeg,* its German *Stuck* (piece). Also used for some fish, *e.g.,* cod steak, salmon steak.

Stearin. The chief constituent of solid fats, such as mutton suet, used for moulding socles, etc.

Stechi, Stehy. A Russian national soup, made of oatmeal.

Sterlet. A fish belonging to the sturgeon family.

Stewed. Etuvé, F.

St. Cloud. A village and ruined castle between Paris and Versailles. A number of dishes are so named.

St. Germain, F. A kind of pear. Also the name of a green pea-soup.

St. Hubert, F. The patron saint of the hunters. Several dishes made with or containing game so named.

Stilton. A well-known and popular English cheese which takes its name from Stilton, a small village on the Great North Road some seventy-five miles from London—where it was sold at the famous Angel Inn which in the old days stabled over 300 horses for coaching and posting purposes.

Stirabout. Name of an Irish dish similar to Scotch porridge.

Stock. Fond, F. The liquid or broth in which meat and bones have been boiled, of which soups and sauces are made.

Stove (to). To heat or bake in a stove or oven.

St. Pierre, F. John Dory, a fish found in British seas. Name derived from the French *jaune dorée* (golden yellow), the body of the fish being thus marked.

Strawberry. Fraise, F. The strawberry has been cultivated in England from a very early period. The strawberry is also found in Asia, Africa, Canada, and the more northern parts of the United States.

Straw Wine. The pressings of grapes which have been dried on straw.

Stuffed. Farci, F.

Sturgeon. A fish of very fine flavour. It was formerly considered exclusively royal property. The roe is made into caviare. It is found in the Caspian, Black, Mediterranean, and Baltic Seas, in the Danube, Volga, Don, some of the large rivers of North America, and occasionally in the Thames, Esk, and Eden. Sturgeon are usually large, some measuring three or four feet in length.

Succotash. An American dish made of green maize and

143

baked beans. The dish is said to be borrowed from the Narraganset Indians, known to them as "Susichquatash."

Succulent, F.   Juicy.

Sucking-pig. Cochon de lait, F.

Suédoise (à la).   Swedish Style.

Sugar. Sucre, F.   Obtained from various plants, more especially from the sugar-cane and the beetroot; but that obtained from other plants is absolutely identical, and differs in no respect from cane or beet sugars after being refined to the same degree of purity as those made from the latter plants. Science described sugar to be a substance sweet to the taste, crystallisable and resolvable by fermentation into carbonic acid and alcohol. Dissolved in water and concentrated by heat we obtain syrups of various degrees according to requirements for culinary purposes. Pounded and sifted it is used for confectionery, pastry, cakes, puddings, etc. The use of sugar in its various forms covers a very extensive field, and its application, it is said, is still capable of further extension. *Sucré,* F.—Sweetened.

Sugar Candy. Alphenic, F.   Is made by suspending strings in a strong solution of sugar, which is left standing in a cool place until the candy is deposited on the strings.

Sugar Pea. A variety of pea cooked and served in their pods, which are destitute of the tough inner lining found in ordinary peas.

Sugee. A species of white grain ground to a powder. It is a most healthy food and is grown in Calcutta. Sugee pudding is in flavour something like semolina or tapioca. It comes from full grained Indian flour. Calcutta bread is made of sugee. It is said that sugee is good for the lungs.

Suif, F.   Mutton suet; tallow.

Suisse (à la).   Swiss Style

Sultane, F.   A West Indian marsh bird. Also applied to a confectionery dish.

Sultanes, F.   Sultanas; small seedless raisins.

Supper. Souper, F.   The last meal of the day.

Suprême, F.   Best; most delicate.

Suprême Sauce. A rich, delicately-flavoured cream sauce, made from chicken stock, etc. *Suprême de Volaille*—breast of chicken entrée.

Surard, F.   Elderberry vinegar.

144

Sureau, F. (*See* ELDERBERRY.). *Graines de sureau,* F.—elderberries. *Vin de sureau,* F.—elderberry wine.

Surlonge, F. (*See* SIRLOIN.)

Suzanne (Alfred), 1829–1917. A French chef, an authority on the culinary treatment of eggs. Author of "Egg Cookery: Over 150 Ways of Cooking and Serving Eggs," and "One Hundred Ways of Cooking Potatoes," also "La Cuisine Anglaise et Patisserie."

Swede or **Swedish Turnip.** A somewhat coarse but excellently flavoured root vegetable of yellowish colour.

Sweetbread. Ris, F. This is the general name for the pancreas of the calf, lamb or any other animal used for food. *Ris de veau*—calf's sweetbread.

Sweet Potato. A vegetable from the West Indies and other tropical countries. It is not allied to the common potato, its name being a corruption of the Portuguese word "batutus."

Syllabub. A kind of milk-punch. Made from milk or cream beaten up with sugar, wine, lemon juice, etc. Also spelt sillabub or sillibub.

Syngnathe. Sangnat, F. A kind of fish sometimes called sea-serpents from their shape.

Syrup. Sirop, F. A saturated solution of sugar, generally flavoured with some fruit essence; used for various culinary purposes.

Tabasco. (*See* TOBASCO.)

Table d'Hôte, F. The table at which the principal meals at an hotel or restaurant are served to guests. A common table for guests. It also serves as a general title for a meal of several courses at a fixed price.

Table Napkin. Serviette, F.

Tafia. A kind of rum. A messenger. A sauce served with brandy made in the West Indies from the sugar-cane.

Tagliarini. A kind of macaroni paste cut in fine shreds.

Tagliati. Nouille paste cut in irregular, extremely thin pieces.

Tailler la Soupe, F. A culinary expression. Thin slices or crusts of bread placed in a soup tureen are called tailles. *Tremper la soupe* is the French term applied when the broth is poured over the slices.

Taillevant. Name of a clever artist in cookery who superintended the kitchens of Charles VII. of France from 1430 to 1461. Invented several dishes including a soup, an omelette, a chicken dish and a method of preparing veal which were later dedicated to Agnès Sorel, mistress of Charles VII.

Talleyrand. Several high-class dishes are styled thus. The name comes from an old French ducal family.

Talleyrand, Marquis de. A French diplomatist who advised Napoleon to rule Europe by its stomach. Himself an epicure whose *chef* was Carême, he never received guests at his table without first visiting the kitchen to see if the preparations for the feast were in order. He introduced the practice of taking cheese with soup into France.

Talmouse, F. A kind of French pastry, sweet or savoury, made in the shape of parsons' caps.

Tamarind. Tamarin, F. The name of a tropical tree and its fruit, which is used for condiments, sauces, etc., largely imported from the East and West Indies. The pulp is used as a laxative and refrigerant.

Tambour, F. A fine sugar sieve. Also name of a small dessert biscuit.

Tamis, F. Tammy. Fine sieve. Woollen canvas cloth used for straining soups and sauces.

Tamisé. Rubbed through a tammy cloth or tammy sieve.

Tanche, F. (*See* TENCH.)

Tansy. A herb with strong aromatic flavour, sometimes used for flavourings in puddings.

Tapioca. A farinaceous food substance. The product of a tree or plant obtained from the roots of the cassava (manioc plant), a native of the tropical parts of Asia, America, and Africa. Brazil exports the most to this country. Tapioca is one of the most easily digested farinaceous foods, and is therefore recommended for invalids and children.

Tari. A liquor obtained from palm trees.

Tarragon. Estragon, F. Aromatic plant used for flavouring; also for flavouring vinegar.

146

Tart. Pie. From the Latin "torta," a baked ring of twisted dough, which was laid round and eaten with cooked fruit. The name now includes a great number of cakes and pastry of a more or less complicated kind.

Tartare, F. A cold sauce, made of yolks of eggs, oil, vinegar, mustard, capers, gherkins, etc., served with fried fish or cold meats; also a salad dressing.

Tartaric Acid. This is an acid which exists in a great many kinds of fruit, though it is chiefly obtained and extracted from the grape root. It is used for similar purposes as citric acid, and has the same effect on sugar.

Tartelette, or **Tourtelette,** F. Tartlet. Small, thin paste crust shapes (round or oval), filled with fruit or other sweet or savoury mixtures.

Tartine, F. A slice of bread. French name for sandwich.

Tartre, F. Tartar; tartaric acid.

Tassajo. A South American name for dried meat or powdered meat.

Tasse, F. Cup. *En tasse*—served in cup.

T-Bone steak. A term used to describe a steak cut from a sirloin of beef including bone. It may be for one, two, or three people and is usually grilled and suitably garnished. (*See* PORTERHOUSE.)

Tea. Thé, F. Tea was introduced into England about the year 1661, when Samuel Pepys writes of drinking it for the first time. In 1663 the East Indian Company presented the king with two pounds of tea, and in 1666 it was sold in London for sixty shillings a pound. The difference between black and green tea is caused by a difference in the method of drying the leaf. Tea is now extensively cultivated in Ceylon, India, and Assam, as well as in China.

Teal. Sarcelle or Cercelle, F. A water-fowl of the duck tribe, whose flesh is of great delicacy, and much esteemed by epicures.

Tench. Tench, F. A fresh-water fish, allied to the carp. Seasonable December to February.

Tendron, F. Tendon; gristle. Piece from the breast of lamb or veal, in which the gristle is found.

Tent. A red wine, chiefly used for sacramental purposes.

Terrapène, F. Terrapin. A small American turtle, very little known or used in this country.

Terrine. China pan or pot, used for pâtés, and for potted meats.

Tête, F. Head. *Tête de moine*—a cheese made in the Jura. Literally "monk's head." *Tête de veau*—calf's head.

Tétragone, F. Tetragonia. New Zealand spinach.

Tétras, F. The French grouse; prairie chicken.

Therid. An Arab word for a soup. Principal ingredients used are: broth, olive oil, eggs, vinegar, and breadcrumbs.

Thermometer. An instrument to ascertain degrees of temperature, oven heat, etc.

Thickening. Liaison, F. A term applied in cookery to the rendering of gravies, soups, or other liquids thicker by the addition of egg yolk or certain farinaceous substances.

Thon, F. Tunny fish. A sea-fish of the mackerel family, usually preserved in oil. *Thon mariné*—pickled tunny fish.

Thousand Island Dressing. A type of dressing for salads.

Thyme. An aromatic plant used for flavouring. Lemon thyme is a species which has a delicate flavour of the lemon, and is used for culinary purposes when this flavour is desired.

Tiburon. Tiburo, a fish of the shark species.

Tiffin. The name given by Anglo-Indians to a light repast taken between ten and eleven o'clock in the morning.

Timbale, F. Literally "kettledrum" or "drinking-cup." The term is now applied to thimble-shaped moulds of savoury preparations of meat, etc. *Moule à timbale,* F.—timbale mould.

Tiré, F. Pulled, as *sucre tiré*—pulled sugar.

Toad-in-the-hole. A typical English dish. Pieces of meat or sausages baked in batter.

Toast. Pain grillé, F. Grilled or toasted slices of bread.

Tobasco. Tabasco. Name of a pungent Indian pepper-sauce.

Tocane. New juice of grapes. New champagne wine in its first stage.

Toddy. An American punch. (An iced fruit drink flavoured with rum.)

Toffee. A sweetmeat originally made in Lancashire.

Tokay. Tokai, F. A Hungarian wine. It is made from grapes called "Hungarian Blue," which are allowed to shrivel in the sun before being gathered. Tokay, when fully matured by keeping, will remain unchanged for a hundred years.

Tom and Jerry. An egg punch; an American drink.

Tomate, F. Tomato. Also called love-apples (pommes

d'amour) from the Italian *pomi di mori* (Moorish apples). The word tomato is said to be derived from the Spanish American name, tamata. The tomato-plant is a native of South America. It was introduced into Europe by the Spaniards in 1583, and into England in 1596; but it is only since the year 1880 that the culture of the tomato has developed into a distinct horticultural industry.

Tomber à Glace, F. To reduce a liquid until it has the appearance of a thick syrup or glaze.

Tonalchile. (*See* GUINEA PEPPER.)

Tonca. Tonca or Tonquin bean.

Tongue. (*See* LANGUE.)

Topinambour, F. (*See* JERUSALEM ARTICHOKE.)

Torte, G. **Tourte,** F. Tart. An open tart baked in a round, shallow tin.

Tortillas. Thin Mexican bread-cakes prepared from yucca or manioc flour.

Tortue, F. Turtle. Also called the sea porpose. (*See* TURTLE.) *Tortue (en)*—turtle garnish. *Tortue-fausse*—mock turtle.

Tortue liée. Thick turtle.

Tortue claire. Clear turtle.

Tôt-fait, F. Flap jack; a pancake.

Toulouse (à la), F. A rich white stew of chicken or veal, mushrooms, truffles, etc., used for filling paste crusts, *bouchées* and *vol-au-vent,* or for garnishing.

Tourné, F. Shaped, cut, soured, curdled, *Tourner,* F.—to stir a sauce; also to pare and cut roots.

Tournedos, F. Small, thin fillets of beef served as entrées. First served in Paris in 1855. The French meaning of tournedos is that it is cooked in a twinkling, or, while, the back of the cook is turned.

Tourterelle, F. Turtle dove.

Tourtière, F. Tart mould; pie dish; baking dish.

Tourtelette, F. (*See* TARTELETTES.)

Traiteur, F. Caterer. Eating-house keeper.

Tranche, F. Slice of meat or fish, melon, bread, cake, etc. *Tranche (en)*—in slices. *Trancher*—to cut or carve.

Trautmannsdorff. Name of an Austrian Count, born 1749, died 1827. Several sweets are styled after his name.

Treacle. A thick, dark-coloured syrup, formed during the manufacture of cane or moist sugar. Its food value is the same as that of sugar.

Treble Palma. The highest grade of quality in sherry.

Tremper la Soupe, F. To pour the soup over thin slices or crusts of bread placed in the soup-tureen.

Trepang. Béche de mer, F. Also called sea slug and sea cucumber. Species of *holothuria* much relished by the Chinese. It lives in the Malay and Australasian seas.

Trianon (à la), F. Trianon style, usually a dish or garnishing in three colours.

Trifle. A dish of sweetmeats and cake. A second course dish of cakes, biscuits, jams, etc.

Trim. To pare; to cut off portions of meat or vegetables in order to improve their appearance.

Tripe. Tripe, F. The inner lining of the stomach of the ox or cow. The best parts are those known as the "blanket" or "double," because folded with fat between the "honey-comb," and the "monkshood," which latter is deeper in colour. When cooked it is very easily digested, and is said to possess great nourishing properties.

Tronçon, F. A slice of flat fish which includes the bone, *e.g.*; turbot—*tronçon de turbot*.

Tronçon de Saumon, F. Middle-cut of salmon.

Trout. Truite, F. A much esteemed fresh-water fish. During the hot weather this fish retires into deep water, where it remains until about the end of September.

Truffle. Truffe, F. A fungus of the same order as the mush-room. They grow in clusters of an irregular globular form under roots of young trees (oak, nut, and a few other trees). There are three kinds: the black, the grey, and the red. The latter is musk-scented, and very rare. The former two are mostly used for garnish and other culinary purposes. The South and West of France produce the best kinds. Trained pigs and dogs are employed to find truffles. Périgueux and Carpentras are the most famous districts in France. *Truffé*—truffled; garnished with truffles. *Truffer*—to garnish a sauce with truffles or to season the interior of poultry or game with truffle-stuffing, such as capons, turkeys, and pheasants.

Truite au Bleu, F. Trout cooked plain in a court bouillon, having been passed through vinegar prior to cooking (immediately after being taken from a trout tank and prepared).

Truite saumonée, F. Salmon trout. *Truitelle*—troutlet, a small trout.

Truss. To tie a bird with string, which is passed through and fastened in such a manner as to keep it in perfect shape during the process of cooking, both roasting and boiling.

Tunny Fish. (*See* THON.)

Turban. Ornamental entrées of chicken and forcemeat, dressed in the form of a turban; a hairdress worn in the East.

Turban of Veal. A cold dish composed of cold cut-up fowl, slices of cold veal garnished with tongue and truffle, the whole arranged in the form of a turban.

Turbit. A variety of the domestic pigeon, having a very short beak.

Turbot. Turbot, F. A highly esteemed flat sea-fish. The flesh of the turbot is firm, white, and delicate in flavour. It is one of the few that improve by keeping for a day or two. Our supply comes principally from the English coasts, and from a few places off the Dutch coast. The turbot of the Adriatic was held in great esteem by the Romans. This fish was called "Phasianus Aquaticus" in the Middle Ages—meaning water pheasant. *Turbotin*—small turbot. *Turbotière*—turbot-kettle or pan in which turbot is cooked.

Turkey. Dinde, Dindon, F. A large species of domestic fowl. Though called "turkey," after the country of that name, it is really a native of North America. It was introduced into Europe by one of Sebastian Cabot's lieutenants in the 16th century and into England in the reign of Henry VIII. Wild turkeys are still found in America, and their flesh has a finer flavour, although a deeper colour, than the domesticated bird. The flavour of a young bird of moderate size is better than that of a large one. The old birds may be known by the roughness and redness of their legs, which in the younger are black and smooth. *Turkey-poult*—dindonneau.

Turkish Delight, or **Rahat Lakoum.** Name given to a delicious sweetmeat or Turkish origin.

Turmeric. Curcuma, F. Powdered turmeric root is the ingredient to which curry-powder owes its colour. Turmeric tubers yield a deep yellow powder of a resinous character. It is a principal ingredient in some Indian dishes.

Turn. Tourner, F. To trim or pare vegetables into neat round or oval shapes.

Turnip. Navet, F. A white bulbous root, said to have been introduced into England from Hanover, as late as the reign of George I. The common variety and the Swede are extensively grown in England. A third variety, long in shape, resembling the carrot, yellowish-white in colour and strong in flavour, was formerly grown here, but is now imported from France.

Turnip-tops. The young leaves of the turnip, especially the Swede, are excellent cooked as a vegetable, although rather pungent and bitter.

Turtle. Tortue, F. Edible marine or sea tortoise. The green turtle is considered the most highly prized as a food delicacy; in addition to the famous turtle soup, numerous other dishes are made from it. The turlte was first brought to England in the middle of the 17th century. Its appearance as an edible dish is at first sight repulsive. At the beginning of the 18th century turtle was only eaten in Jamaica by the poor.

Tutti-frutti. An Italian expression for various kinds of fruits, or a mixture of cooked vegetables. Ice-cream, etc., mixed with different sorts of candied fruits.

Twelfth Cake. A large cake, into which a bean, ring or other article was introduced, made for Twelfth Night festivals. The cake being cut up, whosoever got the piece containing the ring or bean was accepted as king for the occasion.

Tyrolienne, F. A garnish consisting of fried onion rings and *tomates concassées,* applicable to small cuts of meat which have been grilled or sautéed.

Ucha. A Russian fish soup.

Ude (Louis Eustache). A famous chef, at one time cook to Louis XVI. and the Earl of Sefton. Author of the "French Cook," published in 1827.

Umble, F. (*See* OMBLE.)
Umbre, F. (*See* OMBRE.)
Usquebaugh. (*See* WHISKY.)
Uvaggio. Any Italian wine made from mixed grapes.

Vachelin, Vacherin. A Jura cheese; with whipped cream, also name given to an open cheese tart. More commonly known as a sweet consisting of meringue piped in a circle and filled with fruit and cream.

Valence, F. Valencia, a section of Spain famous for its vineyards and its oranges.

Van der Hum. A Cape liqueur not unlike Curaçao, made from the Cape orange or naartje.

Vandreuil, F. An excellent fish, found principally at the seaside of the French Dept. Provence.

Vanille, F. Vanilla. The fruit of a fragrant plant; the most delicate flavouring known, used for all kinds of sweet dishes. It grows principally in Brazil, Guiana, Mexico, and the West Indies.

Vanneau, F. Lapwing; peewit.

Vanner, F. To stir a sauce quickly, so as to work it up lightly, in order to make it smooth. Literally, to winnow.

Vatel. Name of a clever and ingenious chef, who acted in that capacity to Louis XIV. of France. He took his life because the fish for a special banquet did not arrive in time. Died 1671.

Veal Tendon. (*See* TENDRON.)

Veau, F. Veal. The flesh of the calf. *Veau (tête de)*—calf's head.

Vegetables. Légumes, F.

Vegetable-marrow. Courge, F. It grows best in warm or tropical regions, and is largely cultivated in Persia, whence it was introduced into England.

Velouté or **Veloutée,** F. Velvet-like; smooth. A rich white sauce made from chicken stock, cream, etc.; also applied to certain cream soups.

Venaison, F. Venison, the flesh of the deer. During the Middle Ages, when wild animals were more plentiful, venison was more popular than it is now.

Verduresse, F. Green vegetables; salad herbs; pot herbs. A common street cry in Paris.

Verjus, F. Verjuice. Juice of unripe grapes or crab-apples.

Vermicelle, F. Vermicelli, IT. Very fine strings of paste, threadlike in appearance, made from the dough of wheat flour, and forced through cylinders or pipes till it takes a slender, worm-like form, when it is dried; used in soups, puddings, etc.

Vermouth. A favourite aromatic wine distilled from wormwood, sweet wine, and various fruits, herbs, and spices; said to stimulate appetite. The French Vermouth is drier than the Italian.

Vert-pré, F. Name of a green herb sauce, or applied to dishes with green garnishing.

Viande, F. Meat, viands. *Viande de carême*—Lenten food. *Viande faisandée, hasardée*—meat kept till it is high. *Menue viande*—fowl and game.

Vichy, F. A mineral water from springs at Vichy, a French watering-place.

Vichysoisse, F. A cold soup prepared from a *purée Parmentier* mixed with cream and finished with chopped chives.

Vichy, F. A mineral water from springs at Vichy, a French watering-place.

Villeroi, F. Name of a famous French family. Several dishes are so named.

Villeroux. Name of a chef, a friend of the great Carême, who was famous as Count Mirabeau's chef, said to have invented the *Omelette au jambon.*

Vin, F. Wine. *Vin blanc (au)*—done in white wine.

Vinaigre, F. Vinegar. Literally sour wine. *Vin-aigre*—used for pickling, in sauces, and for salads. Vinegar is made from apples, wood, sugar, and from any kind of grain, but chiefly from cheap and inferior wines. Malt forms the chief substance from which the ordinary table vinegar is made in England. *Vinaigre de framboises*—raspberry vinegar. *Vinaigrer*—to season with vinegar. (*See* ACETIC ACID.)

154

Vinaigrette. A salad sauce of vinegar, oil, pepper, and herbs.

Vin D'un Anno. Term applied to young or first year's sherry.

Violette, F. Violet. A dark blue flower, of delicate perfume, of a low, herbaceous plant, used crystallised for sweets, etc.

Vitamins. Name given to an important and vital food element which is primarily in plant life, especially in or just under the husk of rice, wheat, barley, in oranges, tomatoes and all fruits, also in butter and cream, etc.

Vitelotte. Peachblow potato. Red kidney potato.

Vlattero. A Greek liqueur.

Volaille, F. Poultry. Name given collectively to all domesticated birds used as food, including chicken, duck, pigeon, turkey, guinea-fowl, goose, etc.

Vol-au-vent, F. Round or oval case made of puff pastry, filled with a rich ragoût of cooked meat, game, chicken, sweetbread, and sometimes fruit.

Vopallière, F. A dish of small chicken fillets, larded and braised, served with truffle sauce. Name also applied to other dishes.

Vraie Tortue, F. Real turtle. (*See* TURTLE.)

V.S O. Initials used to describe certain brandies as Very Special Old Brandy.

V.S.O.P. Very Special Old Pale Brandy.

Vuillemot. A French chef who owned the *Tête Noir* at St. Cloud; friend and culinary adviser of Alexandre Dumas.

Wafers. (*See* GAUFRES.)

Waffles or Waffeln. (*See* GAUFRES.)

Walnut. Noix, F. Originally imported from Persia, is generally served with fruits as dessert. The unripe fruit is pickled, or made into ketchup.

Wassail or **Wastle Cake.** (Scotch.) Wastle bread was baked on a girdle, which is analogous to the English girdle or griddle cake.

Washington. When this term is used on menus it usually denotes that sweet corn is featured in the dish in some form, often in a cream sauce.

Water. Eau, F. A transparent fluid composed of oxygen and hydrogen. Water cannot be classified as food, for it produces neither heat nor force, though without it all vital action would come to a standstill.

Watercress. Cresson de fontaine, F. An aquatic plant, used for salads, etc. Originally it was found growing wild in our own country, but it has been cultivated since 1808. There are three varieties, the green-leaved, small brown-leaved, and the large brown-leaved, the last named being considered the best.

Water-souchet. Name derived from the Dutch word "Water-zoetje." It is a fish stew served in a souptureen, or vegetable dish. It is eaten with a spoon. (*See also* SOUCHET.)

Wedding Cake. Gâteau de Noce, F.

Welsh Rarebit. Commonly called "Welsh rabbit." A slice of toasted bread covered with melted cheese and butter, seasoned with pepper and mustard.

Whale. A sea animal, whose flesh resembles butcher's meat.

Wheatear or **Clodhopper.** This little bird is highly esteemed for the table, especially in the Sussex watering-places. It is also called Fallowchat.

Whelk. A shellfish most indigestible as a food.

Whey. Petit lait, F. The uncoagulated portion of milk, used as a cooling beverage.

Whipped Cream. Crème fouettée, F.

Whisky, Whiskey. Eau de vie de grain, F. (*Spiritus frumenti* to medical men.) Spelt whisky in Scotland and whiskey in Ireland. Gaelic name Usquebaugh, from *uisge* (water) and *beatha* (life). A spirit made by the distillation of the fermented extract from malted and unmalted cereals, barley, corn, rye, and potatoes, or any other starch-yielding material, but preferably from malted barley.

Whitebait. Blanchaille, F. The smallest known species of the herring genus. When fried they form one of the most appreciated dishes of the *haute cuisine*. Owing to their great delicacy they ought to be cooked as fresh as possible. Slices of lemon and thinly cut brown bread and butter are always handed round with this fish.

Whitepot. An ancient preparation of cream, eggs, pulp of apples, etc., etc., baked in a dish or in a crust. This is a kind of custard fruit purée pie, verging towards a charlotte.

White Stew. (*See* BLANQUETTE.)

Whiting. Merlan, F. Seasonable March to August. This fish is very delicate, and easily digested. It seldom exceeds a pound and a half in weight, or ten or twelve inches in length. In the winter it swarms in large shoals within three miles of the shore for the purpose of depositing its spawn. In the winter time this fish is sometimes sold under the peculiar name of "buckhorn," which is simply whiting caught in Cornwall, salted and dried.

Whortleberry or **Huckleberry.** Airelle Myrtille, F.

Widgeon. Macreuse, F. Seasonable October to February. The widgeon belongs to the same family as the wild duck. Genus *Mareca*. It is a native of the northern regions of Europe and Asia. Early in March they begin their Polar migration. Sometimes incorrectly called *sarcelle* in French, but *sarcelle* is properly the teal.

Wiener Schnitzel, G. A favourite Viennese dish of veal cutlets, garnished with fried yolks of eggs, anchovy fillets, etc., often served with sauerkraut.

Wild Boar. Sanglier, F. The flesh of the wild boar is finer than that of the pig. It is found in the forests and marsh lands of the temperate regions of Europe and Asia. The wild boar seeks its food at night, feeding on roots which it digs up with its snout. Where truffles abound, its flesh obtains a peculiarly delicate flavour.

Wild Duck. Canard sauvage, F. This bird is also called the mallard, and is highly esteemed for the table. It is distinguished from the tame duck by the colour of its feet being red, while those of the tame duck are yellow.

Wild Goose. The flesh of the wild goose has a more gamey flavour than that of the domesticated bird.

Windsor Beans. Called Broad beans.

Wine. Vin, F. The fermented juice of the grape.

Woodcock. Bécasse, F. Seasonable October to December. This bird is celebrated for the exquisite flavour of its flesh. It should be cooked without being drawn, the trail being considered by epicures a great delicacy. When the spring change of plumage commences, the bird loses its delicacy. The woodcock is a native of the northern latitudes of Europe and Asia.

Wood Pigeon. Mansard, F. These birds should be hung for a few days. They may be cooked as ordinary pigeons. (*See* PIGEON.)

Work (to). This expression is frequently used as a culinary term, especially so in connection with sauces, mixtures, batters, creams, or pastes. It indicates that it is to be stirred briskly with a spoon, whisk, or the hand until smooth. In making ices its meaning conveys vigorous stirring with the spatule during the operation of freezing.

Wurst. The German for sausage, fresh or smoked.

Xanthurus. An East Indian fish, resembling the carp; known in the Dutch colonies as *geelstaart* or yellow-tail.

Xavier. Name of a clear soup. Supposed to have been introduced by King Louis XVIII. in honour of Count Xavier of Saxony, who died in 1806.

Xeres (Vin de), F. Sherry. Spanish strong wine of deep amber colour and aromatic flavour; so-called from Xeres, a place near Cadiz.

Xerophagy. The eating of dry meats.

Yak. A species of ox found in Tibet.

Yamadon. An oil from the yellow nutmeg.

Yam. Igname, F. A tropical vegetable similar to the sweet potato.

Yapok, Yapock. The South American water opossum.

Yapon, Yaupon, Yupon. An evergreen shrub whose leaves yield the "black drink" of the Indians.

Yeast. Levain; levure, F. Also called barm. It is added in small quantities to flour for making dough intended to ferment, in order to quicken the process.

Yering. A delicate red dry Australian wine.

Yokola. A Kamtchatka dish.

Yorkshire Pudding. A light baked batter made of flour, eggs, and milk; generally served with roast beef.

Yorkshire Rarebit. A Welsh rarebit (toasted bread and cheese), with a slice of broiled bacon and a poached egg on top.

Young Wild Boar. (*See* MARCASSIN, F.).

Ysard. Chamois of the Pyrenees.

Yucker. The American flicker of golden-winged woodpecker.

Yvette (crême). A liqueur extracted from violets, etc.

Yvorne. An amber sub-acidulous wine; the most highly-prized of Swiss wines, grown in the Yvorne district.

Zabyajone, IT. Zabaglione. A frothing mixture of wine, yolks of eggs, and sugar, thickened over the fire, and served hot in glasses.

Zakuska. The Russian name for *hors d'œuvre*.

Zamia. A genus of palm-like trees, some species of which yield an edible starchy pith.

Zambone, IT. Stuffed and salted pigs' feet.

Zander, Zant, Sander. The European pike perch.

Zea. Botanical name of maize or Indian corn.

Zeltinger. Name of a favourite German white wine. Largely used for cups.

Zéphire, F. Name of small oval-shaped forcemeat dumplings, a kind of quenelles, which are poached and served with a rich sauce. Anything shaped in a zephire mould.

Zeste, F. Zest. The outer skin of the orange or lemon, cut thinly; also the skin covering the kernel of a walnut. *Zesté*—flavoured with the outer skin of the orange or lemon.

Zingel, G. A fish of the perch family, found in the Danube.

Zi⁺anie. Wild rice. A Canadian variety is cultivated by the North-American Indians.

Zedoary. A powerful sudorific; a bitter pungent root of the turmeric family grown in India and China.

Zein. A protein found in Indian corn.

Zuchetti, Zucchini, IT. As for courgette (*q.v.*).

Zuppa al Brodo. A fish broth with toasted bread and cheese. (Italian.)

Zwieback, G. Toasted or twice baked milk bread or cake. Literally, twice baked. Also a whole-grain flour crispbread.

Zymology. The doctrine of fermentation of liquors.

Zymometer. An instrument for measuring the degree of fermentation of liquids.

Zythogala. Græcified name applied by Sydenham, the English physician, and later by the French doctor, Secquet, to the then popular posset.

Zythos. A kind of beer made by the ancient Egyptians.

Zythum. A liquid made from malt and wheat.

METRIC MEASUREMENT

In 1965 it was announced in Parliament that a gradual process of metrication would be introduced in this country. It was anticipated that by 1975 the process would be almost complete. This means that we are having to get used to a different system of measurement. The system, although referred to as a change to metric measurement is really a change to SI (Système Internationale). This means using a selection of metric units which are used throughout the world.

Those which concern us most are:—

Length:—kilometre (km), metre (m), millimetre (mm).
Area:—square kilometre (km²), hectare (h), square metre (m²).
Mass, i.e.:—weight—tonne (t), kilogramme (kg), gramme (g).
Volume:—litre (l), cubic metre (m³).
Temperature:—degree Celsius (°C).
Time:—second (s) (24 hour clock).

SI Preferred units are $10^{\pm 3}$, i.e.: thousands or thousandths of the basic unit, i.e.: kilogrammes—grammes, litres—millilitres, kilometre—millimetres, etc.

Some examples of equivalents are given below.

Capacity:

¼ pt = 142 ml
½ pt = 284 ml
¾ pt = 426 ml
1 pt = 568 ml
½ litre = 0.88 pint.
1 litre = 1.76 pints.

Mass:

1 oz = 28.35 g
2 ozs = 56.7 g
4 ozs = 113.4 g
6 ozs = 170.10 g
8 ozs = 226.8 g
12 ozs = 340.2 g
16 ozs = 453.6 g
2 lbs. = 906 g
2.2 lbs. = 100 g = 1 kg

Temperature:

 32°F=0° Celsius
212°F=100°C
225°F=107°C
250°F=121°C.
275°F=135°C.
300°F=149°C.
325°F=163°C.
350°F=177°C.
375°F=190°C.
400°F=204°C.
425°F=218°C.
450°F=232°C.
500°F=260°C.

To convert Fahrenheit to Celsius subtract 32 and multiply by $\frac{5}{9}$.

TABLE OF TEMPERATURE EQUIVALENTS
FOR OVEN THERMOSTAT MARKINGS

Description	Gas Regulo	Fahrenheit	Celsius
		150°F	70°C
		175°F	80°C
		200°F	100°C
		225'°F	110°C
very cool	¾	250°F	130°C
very cool	½	275°F	140°C
cool	1–2	300°F	150°C
warm	3	325°F	170°C
moderate	4	350°F	180°C
fairly hot	5	375°F	190°C
fairly hot	6	400°F	200°C
hot	7	425°F	220°C
very hot	8	450°F	230°C
very hot	9	475°F	240°C
		500°F	250°C

It can be seen from the above that the strict metric equivalents, although acting as a rough guide, are not very useful for practical purposes, especially for capacity and mass; the weights are difficult to measure accurately and are not used in ordinary cooking.

One alternative is to use 25 grammes as the unit for 1 oz (dry ingredients); this is being adopted in many schools and colleges throughout the country and by many authors of recipe books.

Reasons put forward for the adoption of a basic unit of 25 g are that it can easily be multiplied for larger quantities up to 100–250–500 etc. Many recipes are based on portions of ingredients and 25 g can be easily used in this connection.

It can provide a useful foundation on which to build for the period beyond conversion, e.g.: 100 g as an alternative to 4 ozs provided that account is taken of a difference of minus 12½% in total yield; an important factor regarding costs and portion control.

The preferred units for capacity are the litre (l) and the millilitre (ml) but in view of the difficulties of recipes balance and measurement in some cases, authors are also using the decilitre ($\frac{1}{10}$ of a litre). The problem of recipes containing liquid is one that therefore needs consideration. There are many areas where experienced chefs estimate quantities rather than measuring them accurately and this practice will doubtless continue irrespecitve of which measurements are being used. Nevertheless there are many instances where accuracy is important, especially in pastry work. Because of this, all recipes must be tested before conversion.